☛ WELFARE:
A HANDBOOK FOR
FRIEND AND FOE

☞ WELFARE:
A HANDBOOK FOR
FRIEND AND FOE

BY TIMOTHY J. SAMPSON

A PILGRIM PRESS BOOK FROM
UNITED CHURCH PRESS · PHILADELPHIA

Library of Congress Cataloging in Publication Data

Sampson, Timothy J.   1935-
    Welfare: a handbook for friend and foe.
    "A Pilgrim Press Book."
    Includes bibliographical references.
    1. Public welfare—United States. I. Title.
HV91.S24   361.6'0973   72—8551
ISBN 0-8298-0255-X

United Church Press
1505 Race Street
Philadelphia, Pennsylvania 19102

For my father, who has looked after my welfare, taught me to care about the welfare of others, and shared with me his anger about what is

and for my wife who has helped me begin to find out about my own welfare and to temper my anger with love.

☛ CONTENTS

☛ FOREWORD

The first time I met Tim Sampson was at a university seminar in Washington, D.C. in 1966. As assistant to the United States Commissioner of Welfare in the Department of Health, Education, and Welfare, I was there to explain welfare. The university had also invited a representative of "the people" from the Poverty/Rights Action Center, a bearded activist named Timothy J. Sampson.

I came prepared to debate with this representative of "the other side." Then Tim made his presentation. He was so well informed, and his criticisms of welfare so accurate, that I found myself reduced to the role of confirming what he had already said. Upon further acquaintance, I found that he was a professional social worker and a warm and gracious human being (when he was not playing the role of provocateur).

Four years later, we met again. I was now General Secretary for health and welfare in the United Church of Christ Board for Homeland Ministries, and chairman of its Welfare Priority Team, which was set up to work toward the improvement of the welfare system. Tim was liaison to the team from the National Welfare Rights Organization. He emerged within our group as a natural leader intellectually, strategically, and spiritually. The latter is noteworthy in light of his professed absence of formal religious identification. He was still warm and gracious (when not playing the role of provocateur). I again found myself in the role of confirming the accuracy of Tim's factual statements.

Then Tim returned to the more conventional, professional role of university professor. This time, I worked with him as an author. I am still finding myself in the role of saying, "Yes, he's right." And he is still, as the reader will find, warm and gracious (when not playing the role of provocateur).

I have read all drafts of the book carefully. We have argued a few points. To the best of my knowledge, all facts in this book are accurate and reliable. Most of them come from footnoted official sources. His perspectives and interpretations are soundly based in his research of welfare history and philosophy as well as his own personal experiences. They are plausible, persuasive, and sometimes deliberately provocative. The reader must decide for himself whether they are also true. I think they are.

Why this book? Two reasons. One is that we could not find within one cover any publication which deals comprehensively with the immensely complex United States system of public assistance (alias "relief" or "welfare") in a form that any ordinary person can read and understand. I find this book profound enough to be stimulating to an "old pro" like me. At the same time, I think it is simple enough for laymen (church discussion groups, civic organizations, concerned individual citizens of all persuasions, local groups of welfare recipients, etc.), and comprehensive enough to be a useful text in social policy courses in both undergraduate colleges and graduate schools of social work, as well as in orientation programs for new workers in public welfare departments.

The second reason for such a book is that welfare is a major problem in American society today. Everyone—radicals and reactionaries, conservatives and liberals, welfare administrators and recipients, agree that the present welfare system is unsatisfactory. The system does not provide enough for poor persons to live with any semblance of adequate housing, nutrition, health or dignity. The way in which it is administered under existing laws and regulations frequently breaks up families, fosters dependency, and destroys the spirit and self-respect of those who must accept welfare to survive. Poor people are being hurt! And the rest of us are unhappy with the system too.

Our welfare problems and attempts at solutions are exacerbated by the huge amount of misinformation current in our society. Malicious lies and slanders, some of them put forth by national leaders, confuse the issue. Sincere misconceptions about welfare and welfare recipients are almost universal among citizens of goodwill. Even where accurate information is available, there are many differences in both welfare philosophy and practical proposals for the reform of the inadequate existing system.

Read this book. Get your facts straight. Think about the issues and problems. Decide as best you can how we should improve upon it. And most of all, in Tim's favorite words, **DO IT.**

The format of the book is easily followed. It is desirable to read it straight through, but it is possible to select various chapters for special attention or discussion.

Chapter 1 leads us through the Rube Goldberg contraption which has been our federal/state/local welfare program since 1935.

Chapter 2 is the most concise summary I have ever seen of the historical and philosophical background of the existing welfare program, which has its roots solidly planted in the economic and social assumptions of sixteenth-century England as it was moving from feudalism to a modern capitalist economy.

Chapter 3 gives us facts, facts, facts, about who is on welfare, where, why, how much it costs, who pays, and how well welfare recipients live compared to the rest of us.

Chapter 4 discusses "myths" (hostile allegations about welfare recipients) and "countermyths" (sympathetic allegations about recipients). The author raises key issues of fact and values but leaves it to the reader to make his own judgments. He does, however, give clues and references on how to get further information and additional viewpoints.

Chapter 5 is the most speculative and, for me, the most stimulating part of the book. At this point the book moves from facts to a different, and less statistical attempt to find "truth." It explores the questions, "What is our present welfare system **really** intended to do? What are its **actual** consequences?"

Chapters 6 and 7 discuss serious legislative proposals during 1971 and 1972, plus widely discussed alternatives to the present system and proposed changes. By the time this volume is off the press, there may or may not be major new welfare legislation on the books, but it is absolutely safe to say that the "problem" will not have been "solved" and that the basic issues and alternatives will still be before us.

Chapter 8 leaves the reader with the question, "What are **you** going to do about it?" By the way, what **are** you going to do about it?

HOBART A. BURCH
General Secretary, Division of Health and Welfare
United Church Board for Homeland Ministries

☞ ACKNOWLEDGMENTS

I gratefully acknowledge the help and support I received from:

the Welfare Priority Team of the Board for Homeland Ministries of the United Church of Christ who conceived this project and made it possible

the rank and file members of the National Welfare Rights Organization, their leaders, Mrs. Johnnie Tillmon and Mrs. Beulah Sanders, and also George Wiley and unsung members of the NWRO staff, all of whom helped provide my compensatory welfare education

my father, Jerome N. Sampson, who was a co-organizer of this project and who helped me with it in a great many ways

my wife and children, for love and kindness while I worked on this book

all the Enfield Lintons for the summer it got written

☞ INTRODUCTION

This book grew out of my finding out about the welfare system and trying to figure out what to do about it. I haven't finished either finding out or figuring out what to do so it will not be a blueprint, textbook, or tightly reasoned argument for my point of view.

But it will be **from** my point of view, out of my experience. And you are entitled, I believe, to know in front where I am coming from.

I am a white, male American, thirty-seven years old, married with two children. I am a second generation social worker. My father has held high-level positions in public welfare. My wife worked as a child welfare worker in a county welfare department to put me through school. I worked in a welfare department only between my first and second years of graduate school. I have my master's degree in social work.

My life experience includes: serving as a social work technician in an army prison after being drafted (between Korea and Vietnam); work with emotionally disturbed and delinquent youth while studying social work at the University of Southern California on a National Institute of Mental Health traineeship; three years as a neighborhood organization worker at the Avalon-Carver Community Center in Los Angeles' black community; two years work in community development in rural California including work in support of United Farm Workers Union during the early days of the grape strike; three and one-half years as a staff member of the National Welfare Rights Organization; and two years teaching community organization in the Department of Social Work Education, San Francisco State College.

If asked about my politics I would say that (a) I have none (unfortunately), (b) I **was** a liberal Democrat, and (c) I am on my way toward becoming an American radical.

Although I may **seem** very definite, outspoken, and opinionated, I subscribe to the Saul Alinsky doctrine that more harm has been done in the name of the way, the truth, and the light than in the name of evil! And I am clear that I do **not** have the truth.

I describe my style as DO IT! For me "dissonance not harmony is the music of democracy."

One problem this book may have is like the story of the little boy who went to the library and asked the librarian if she had a book about spinach. She did and was pleased to get it for him. When he returned it a few days later she asked if he had enjoyed it. "No Ma'am," he replied. When asked why not, he said, "That book told me more about spinach than I care to know." I hope this book will **not** be like that for you. If so, I can only fall back on the familiar "Eat it, it's good for you, it will make you grow."

I use humor to stay alive and to temper my anger. I have learned a great deal from writing this book. Those of you who already know some of what I am just finding out may feel at times that I am talking down, putting you on, or trying to contrive something. Not so.

At times it may seem to some of you that I am implying that there is a conspiracy operating with regard to welfare. The only conspiracy of which I am certain is that of silence. You can go from Head Start through a Ph.D. and never have any course about the American welfare system. I wrote this book because there wasn't one like it available.

One final note: This book probably ought to have been published several years ago when welfare began (again) to be an important national issue. Nineteen sixty-seven would have been a good year, 1970 would have been even better, and 1971 might have been the best year in recent times. Had this book been available then, I'm sure its wonderful ideas would have undoubtedly influenced public policy and changed the course of history. However, it was written at a time when the President called welfare reform his number one domestic priority, when Gov. Ronald Reagan of California called welfare the greatest problem he faced as a public official, and when everybody seemed to be aware of and talking about welfare.

It will be published just after the 1972 Presidential Campaign—in which welfare has already emerged as a key issue. So it seems clear that we are still right in the midst of welfare as an important national concern.

But it seems unlikely that we will have heard the end of welfare as an important national issue.

On the National Archives building in Washington, D.C. it says: "All Past Is Prologue." When someone asked Carl Sandburg what that meant he said, "You Ain't Seen Nothin' Yet!" I think that applies to welfare.

If so, then this book may help us "get our heads together." I hope so.

☞ HOW TO SPEAK
WELFARE (a glossary)

WELFARE	Money payments to certain poor people (also called relief, public assistance, public aid, public charity, the dole, the rolls). (Do not confuse with **subsidy** which refers to similar payments made to most nonpoor people.) Welfare payments are sometimes referred to as grants, checks, vouchers, or benefits.
AFDC	Aid to Families with Dependent Children (formerly ADC)
OAA	Old Age Assistance
APTD	Aid to the Permanently and Totally Disabled
AB	Aid to the Blind
AABD	Aid to the Aged, Blind, and Disabled All of these are the federally aided **categories** of welfare (called the **categorical** aid programs). The federal government provides **grants-in-aid** to the states for these programs. OAA, APTD, AB (or the combined AABD) are referred to as the **adult** programs.
MEDICAID	Medical care for poor people usually paid directly to doctor, hospital, lab (called **vendor** payment) under **Title 19** of Social Security Act. **Not** the same as **Medicare,** the medical insurance plan for old people on Social Security.

STATE PLAN	To receive federal funds for all these programs states must (for each category) prepare a **state plan** describing the way they will run the program. If a state violates any federal regulations, they may be declared **out of conformity** and federal funds withheld.
HEW	Department of Health, Education, and Welfare
SRS	Social and Rehabilitation Service
APA	Assistance Payments Administration
CSA	Community Services Administration
NCSS	National Center for Social Statistics
	These are the federal agencies with responsibility for welfare. NCSS, CSA, APA are units of SRS, which is a major unit of HEW. The Department of Labor (DOL) and its Bureau of Labor Statistics (BLS) also relate to welfare. DOL is responsible for the Work Incentive Program (WIN)—work training and job placement services for welfare recipients. BLS compiles information on the cost of living.
WD	Welfare Department
CWD	County Welfare Department
SWD	State Welfare Department
	These may have other names involving public aid, public welfare, public assistance, public charity, social services, etc.

When a poor person applies for welfare he is called an **applicant** and given an **intake** interview to determine if he is **eligible** for welfare. Sometimes he fills out a form stating his eligibility called a **declaration** or a **simplified** eligibility check. Eligibility is periodically **reaffirmed.** Once eligible the poor person becomes a **recipient** or **client.** His **budget** (amount of payment) is figured by subtracting any available **resources** (real or personal property, cash, income, etc.) from the **standard of need**—the amount set by the state as the minimum needed by a family or person in that circumstance. Standard of need minus available resources equals **unmet need** (all or usually some of) which then becomes the welfare grant. This procedure is the **means test.** Once on welfare, the recipient is usually assigned from an intake worker to an **approved** worker. Each case is numbered and each worker has a **file** of cases. Workers, often called social workers or caseworkers, also may try to help the recipient with other problems, such as marital or parent-child problems, housing, health, legal, employment. Help of this kind (versus money) is called **services** or social services. It may involve **counseling** with the recipient, **referral** to other agencies, etc.

When someone is a full-time low-paid worker but still eligible for welfare, the payment may be called a **wage supplement.** The idea that those on welfare should receive less than the lowest-paid worker is called **less eligibility.** When welfare recipients are allowed to keep some portion of income from full- or part-time work instead of 100 percent of it being subtracted from their welfare grant, it is called a **work incentive.** Actually the more correct name for this is **earnings disregard** (or income disregard) since a portion of earnings is **disregarded** in computing the welfare grant (under current law this is **"30 and one third,"** the first $30 and one third of the rest). Certain kinds of income may be designated as **exempt**—not to be counted in determining the welfare payment.

FAP   Family Assistance Program
OFF   Opportunities for Families
      The two components of the current Nixon-Mills welfare reform plan, OFF for families with a member who is judged to be "employable," FAP for families without an employable member.

☞ CHAPTER ONE
STRUCTURE:
WHAT IS WELFARE AND HOW DOES IT WORK?

When we say "on the welfare" and the "welfare system," what do we mean? What are we talking about?

Well, first of all, we do **not** mean the great variety of government subsidies and tax deductions that serve the welfare of most nonpoor people in this country. Those programs—oil depletion allowances, farm subsidies, soil bank payments, FHA loans, mortgage interest tax deductions—are not **called** welfare.*

Neither do we refer to the health and welfare funds of unions or to family and child welfare services. The whole network of service programs usually called "social welfare" is not what we are talking about either.

We are not talking about Social Security, and for our purposes are not even going to talk much about such poor-people-related programs as the War on Poverty or even such directly-related-to-welfare programs as food stamps, surplus commodities, and school lunches or Medicaid.

We are going to stick primarily to the main program which provides **money** directly to poor families. This program is called Aid to Families with Dependent Children (AFDC). It used to be ADC—the **F** was added in 1962. As of January 1972, 10.7

---

* See for example the discussion and "checklist" of such subsidies on pp. 40–42.

million Americans received assistance under AFDC. This was 72% of all those receiving public assistance.

Old people (over 65) receiving Old Age Assistance accounted for 13% more of the total number of persons on welfare as of January 1972, and together AFDC and OAA account for 80% of the cost of welfare payments.

AFDC is one of four federal welfare **categories.** The federal government provides grants-in-aid to the states for four categories of people in need: old people, Old Age Assistance (OAA); blind people, Aid to the Blind (AB); disabled people, Aid to the Permanently and Totally Disabled (APTD); and dependent children (AFDC). AB, APTD, and OAA often are called the adult categories to distinguish them from AFDC, which, despite the fact that it includes parents, is called a "children's" program. Since 1962 states may choose to combine aid to the aged, blind, and disabled in one category (Aid to the Aged, Blind and Disabled— AABD). Nineteen states now do so.

In addition to these four federally aided categories, almost all states and localities provide some aid to people who do not fit into any of these categories; that is, who are not old, blind, disabled, or a dependent child deprived of parental support by reason of the death, physical or mental incapacity, continued absence from the home, or unemployment of a parent. This aid is variously called general assistance (GA), general relief (GR), home relief, county aid, etc. It is a relatively small program (about 1 million versus 10.7 million receiving AFDC) and is supported and controlled either entirely by local government or by some combination of state and local government. Seventeen states administer GA directly. In 17 other states, local political jurisdictions run the program with no state involvement. In the remaining states, there is state supervision or participation. In 17 states GA is totally state-funded, in 17 states there is no state financial participation, and in 16 states the state and local governments share GA costs.

No federal funds are provided for GA, and there are no federal regulations and requirements for it.

Now, with AFDC as our focus, let us look at the legal and administrative framework of welfare. A primary source of complexity in the welfare system is the fact that it is a federal-state-local system with layers of law, regulation, and administration at each level of government.

FEDERAL

The federal law creating our present welfare system is the Social Security Act of 1935 (Public Law 271, 74th Congress 49 Stat. 620 as amended in 1939, 1946, 1950, 1952, 1954, 1956, 1957, 1958, 1959, 1960, 1961, 1962, 1967, 1970).

As its broad description in the law tells, it is an Act:

> To provide for the general welfare by establishing a system of federal old age benefits, and by enabling the several states to make more adequate provision for aged persons, blind persons, dependent and crippled children, maternal and child welfare, public health, and the administration of their unemployment laws; to raise revenue; and for other purposes.

The Social Security Act is an omnibus law which contains the basic federal provisions of the program called Social Security (Old Age, Survivor, Disability and Health Insurance Benefits [OASDHI]); and unemployment compensation as well as for the four public assistance categories.

The provisions of federal law creating and defining AFDC are found in Title IV of the Act, "Grants to the States for Aid and Services to Needy Families with Children. . . ." This provides that the federal government will provide grants to the states:

> For the purpose of encouraging the care of dependent children in their own homes or in the homes of relatives by enabling each state to furnish financial assistance and rehabilitation in such state, as far as practicable under the conditions in such state, to needy dependent children and the parents or relatives with whom they are living to help maintain and strengthen family life and to help such parents or relatives to attain or retain capability for the maximum self-

support and personal independence consistent with the maintenance of continuing parental care and protection, there is
hereby authorized to be appropriated for each fiscal year a
sum sufficient to carry out the purposes of this part. The
sums made available under this section shall be used for
making payments to States which have submitted, and had
approved by the Secretary of Health, Education, and Welfare,
State plans for aid and services to needy families with children.

In order to receive federal funds for this purpose a state
must submit a state plan for AFDC which meets all the basic
federal conditions. There are now twenty-three conditions of
which the most important are that the state plan must:

1. Be in effect in all political subdivisions of the state; that is,
    be statewide.
2. Provide for financial participation by the state.
3. Provide a single state agency to either administer or
    supervise the plan.
4. Provide opportunity for a fair hearing before the state
    agency for any individual whose claim for aid is denied.
5. Provide for administration by personnel employed on a
    merit (civil service) basis.
6. Agree to provide the federal agency with necessary re-
    ports.
7. In determining need take into consideration any other in-
    come and resources (this is the means test provision).
8. Safeguard and restrict use of information concerning re-
    cipients and applicants.
9. Provide that all individuals wishing to apply shall have
    opportunity to do so and that aid be furnished with rea-
    sonable promptness to all eligible individuals.
10. Require notification of appropriate law enforcement offi-
    cial (NOLEO) when aid is given because of parental de-
    sertion.

The states are also required to make **money payments** (versus aid "in kind"), except in certain very specific situations.

The revenue-raising aspects of Social Security mean that legislation regarding it (and by extension and tradition, welfare) must originate in the House of Representatives. Such legislation is the province of the House Ways and Means Committee. In the Senate, welfare legislation is similarly assigned to the Senate Finance Committee (instead, for example, of to the Labor and **Welfare** Committee).

Since 1967, administration of AFDC at the federal level has been the responsibility of the Social and Rehabilitation Service (SRS) of the U. S. Department of Health, Education, and Welfare (HEW). SRS promulgates the federal regulations which spell out the details of the requirements states must meet to receive federal funds. Since 1967 these regulations are adopted pursuant to the procedures of the Code of Federal Regulations (CFR) and published in the Federal Register (see CFR Title 645, chapter 2). SRS is responsible for approving state plans, enforcing federal regulations and law, and for research and reporting to Congress on the operation of federal public assistance programs.

STATE

AFDC as a **federal** program is best described as a grant-in-aid program to the states. Within the federal conditions and regulations described above each state establishes its own AFDC program. **There is thus not one AFDC program but fifty different ones!**

State legislatures adopt statutes establishing an AFDC program and designating a state agency (e.g., a State Department of Welfare) to be responsible for AFDC.

In about half the states AFDC is directly administered by the state. In the rest of the states the state welfare department supervises local government units (usually **counties** but sometimes **cities**) which directly administer AFDC. Even where the state administers AFDC, county government still may be involved.

For example, in Michigan, where the state administers AFDC, there is still a county Social Services Board with two members appointed by the County Board of Supervisors and one by the State Welfare Director who also appoints the County Welfare Director. In Pennsylvania, County Boards of Assistance are appointed by the governor with the advice and consent of the Senate, and the county board chooses the county director.

The state welfare department adopts its own regulations spelling out how, in accord with federal law and regulation and within the state law, welfare is to be administered. These regulations and directives usually are collected into a state welfare manual.

HOW IS AFDC SET UP IN YOUR STATE?

STATE ADMINISTRATION

Directly (20)

Alaska	Nevada
Connecticut	New Hampshire
Delaware	New Mexico
(D.C.)	(Puerto Rico)
Florida	Rhode Island
(Guam)	South Dakota
Hawaii	Texas
Idaho	Utah
Kentucky	Vermont
Maine	(Virgin Islands)
Massachusetts	Washington
Missouri	West Virginia

Through County or Other Local Government (9)

Arizona	Mississippi
Arkansas	Oklahoma
Illinois	Pennsylvania
Louisiana	Tennessee
Michigan	

STATE SUPERVISION

County (or City or other local governmental unit)
Administers AFDC (21)

Alabama	New Jersey
California	New York
Colorado	North Carolina
Georgia	North Dakota
Indiana	Ohio
Iowa	Oregon
Kansas	South Carolina
Maryland	Virginia
Minnesota	Wisconsin
Montana	Wyoming
Nebraska	

Source: SRS/APA,
Public Assistance Report #50,
1970 Edition,
Characteristics of State Plans
Under the Social Security Act.

LOCAL

At the **local** level (unless the state administers welfare directly itself through **state** branch or district welfare offices) welfare is most often the province of county government. Frequently there is some kind of welfare board. In most instances the only local **law** which applies to AFDC is that creating the county welfare department and board and specifying the procedures for selecting the director. However, local welfare departments do develop their own local regulations, procedures, manuals, and forms, further spelling out just how welfare is to be administered. Ordinarily these materials are in direct response and relation to corresponding state regulations and directives.

COSTS

As you may already expect, the sharing of costs among three

levels of government is also complicated. However, there are several key principles:

1. The federal government pays 50% of all administrative costs.
2. The federal government pays 75% of all social service costs.
3. The state must participate financially—it may not simply pass the full nonfederal share of assistance on to the local government.
4. The federal share of assistance varies in relation to the amount of assistance paid, state fiscal effort, and the pattern in other federal/state welfare programs.

On the **average,** the federal government pays about 56%, the state 33% and the local government 11% of AFDC costs. However, the **range** is federal 45% to 79%, state 16% to 55%, local none to 24%.

SERVICES
This is probably a good point at which to make clear the difference **and** relationship between "services" and assistance. As the next chapter makes clear, the ideas of giving poor people money and helping them cope with the myriad of other problems which may or may not have anything to do with why they are on welfare and helping them become "unpoor" (or at least off welfare) have always been entwined.

The most recent confusion came with the 1956, 1962, and 1967 Amendments to the Social Security Act. In these amendments services to AFDC families were first recognized (1956), then encouraged (1962), and then required (1967). Since the federal government agreed to pay 75 percent of the costs of services in 1962 (versus only 50 percent of the cost of administering the aid) the states had a strong incentive to **define** most of what they did with families as "service" (versus just "administration").

However, since services clearly did not fulfill the rosy prom-

A DO-IT YOURSELF WELFARE ORGANIZATION CHART

FEDERAL	STATE	LOCAL
House of Representatives	☐ administers	Name of department
Ways and Means Committee	☐ supervises	
Chairman: Wilbur Mills (D. Ark.)		
Washington, D.C. 20515	Name of department	address
(202) 225-3625		
Senate		phone
Finance Committee	address	
Chairman: Russell B. Long (D. La.)		Director
Washington, D.C. 20510	phone	Other contacts
(202) 225-4515		
Department of Health, Education, and Welfare (HEW)	State Director	
Elliott Richardson, Secretary	Key state legislative contacts	
Social and Rehabilitation Service (SRS)	Chairmen of legislative committees responsible for welfare	
John D. Twiname, Administrator		
330 C Street, S.W.		
Washington, D.C. 20201		
(202) 963-1110		
Assistance Payments Administration		
Commissioner		
Community Services Administration		
Commissioner		
Your HEW regional office		
address city		
phone		
SRS Regional Commissioner		

ises made in their behalf in 1962; that is, not enough people were "rehabilitated" or "serviced" **off** welfare, and because even social workers began to understand the differences and appropriate relationships between the money or "income maintenance" function of welfare and the role of social services, another trend began to separate services from assistance. This is reflected by the organization of the federal agency SRS into an Assistance **Payments** Administration (APA) and a Community **Services** Administration (CSA) and at the local level with the hiring of nonsocial work "eligibility workers" to handle the detail and paper work of applications, recertifying eligibility, and computing budget changes. These workers are then complemented by "service workers" with what can be termed a more traditional social work helping orientation.

HOW WELFARE WORKS

Now by way of illustration and review let's run through a case example and see how welfare works. (This is at least how welfare is **supposed** to work.)

If you are applying for AFDC you are probably a mother (or soon to become one). Your child(ren) must be deprived of parental support by reason of death, physical or mental incapacitation, continued absence from the home, or (since 1961 and in **some states only**) unemployment (of the **father**).

You go to the local welfare office—your county welfare department or closest branch of the state welfare department. You will likely be seen by the eligibility worker assigned to do intake. You will be asked where you reside, when and where your children were born, who their father is and how long and why he is absent from the home (or unemployed). You will be required to cooperate with the Welfare Department in notifying local law enforcement officials of the probable whereabouts of your children's father and you will be asked to assist in his prosecution for nonsupport (if this be the case).

In determining your eligibility (and the size of your welfare grant) the Welfare Department will need to know of **any** income you (or the child) have from any source and also know the value of any real or personal property you may have. Presuming you have little or no income and that your real and personal property is below limits established by your state you will be found eligible and get "on" welfare.

All statements that you give are subject to investigation and verification. Your own parents may be held liable for your support or at least the Welfare Department may ask them if they are able to support you. The Welfare Department may (but does not have to) choose to have you "declare" all this information to be true on a "simplified" form or declaration and then routinely investigate a small sample of such declarations.

They may also **presume** you to be eligible and aid you immediately (but this also is not required). They must, under federal regulation, allow you to apply and act promptly (within thirty days) on your application.

If you are denied aid, not allowed to apply, given less than you think you are entitled to, or treated differently from others in similar circumstances in your state you are entitled to appeal and receive a fair hearing, before an "impartial" person from the state welfare agency.

Once you are on AFDC your case will usually be assigned to an "approved" file and you will ordinarily have a service worker who will talk with you about a "plan" for helping you become self-sufficient again and/or attempt to deal with problems you have (or the worker thinks you have).

The service worker will be responsible for deciding if you are employable and should be referred to the local Employment Service for training or job placement services.

You may or may not find out what medical care you and/or your children are entitled to and likewise you may or may not be given information about food stamps or surplus commodities available to welfare recipients in your county.

If you should go to work or receive any income from any source you will generally be allowed to keep only part of this money. Your budget will be figured by first looking at a table of what a family of your size, composition, and situation (rent, etc.) needs, then from this total there will be subtracted any available income, and you will be entitled to the difference **unless** (and this is **usually** the case) the state has a fixed maximum or percentage it pays instead of what is recognized as your real need! *

As noted above, typically 75 percent of your service worker's salary is paid by the federal government (and 50 percent of all administrative costs). Your workers have been hired under civil service or a state merit system. Service workers have a usual case load of sixty to a hundred families and eligibility workers may have several hundred families.

About six workers (or as many as eight) make up a "unit" which has a supervisor and a clerk. Groups of units make up a district office or welfare center which usually has a director. "Downtown" there is the county administration which includes "middle-management," special investigation and fraud units (these may be directly attached to the district attorney's office), property units (to check on real and personal property), child welfare and foster home placement units, etc. The county welfare director is either responsible to the county board of supervisors or to a county welfare board appointed by elected county or state officials.

Any unusual facet of your case will go up the line for approval—from your worker to the supervisor to the district director, AFDC chief, etc.

In some counties special items of need (a refrigerator, furniture for a family who has lost theirs in a fire, for example) may be provided out of local funds with the proper approvals. Some states provide money for some of these special needs items. In many states recipients get only the "flat" monthly grant—no exceptions or adjustments for special needs.

Through routine state-case sampling (this is called "quality control") the state attempts to **supervise** the county to insure the uniform statewide administration of aid required under federal regulation. Your individual case might thus come to the attention of the state welfare department. Usually, however, you

* For a sample of information provided to aid applicants see pp. 42–44.

will just be a case number and a grant statistic to the state. In any event all you are likely to be to the federal government is a tiny part of the average grant payment made to all the families receiving AFDC the previous quarter, which is the basis for the quarterly federal advance payments to the state.

If there is some controversy attached to a particular state practice and question is raised about whether the state is obeying federal laws and regulations, then the federal government may hold a hearing to decide if the state is "out of conformity." The SRS administrator decides this and, if he so finds, must then cut off federal assistance to the state for that program.

This has been rarely even raised. Very few such hearings have been held and no state has ever been cut off.

So, ordinarily the SRS just sends out new regulations and information about changes Congress makes in the law and then approves the changes states make in the state plan describing how welfare is supposed to work in that state. The SRS also collects statistics about how many people are getting on and off and how much money they get, etc.

However, SRS does maintain staff in all HEW regional offices which can provide useful information and help in efforts to get states to comply with federal regulations.

☞ DO-ITS

(ideas for making this book come alive, if it hasn't already; sources of additional information; etc.)

1. Write your U. S. Senator or Congressman for a copy of the Social Security Act as amended to date. This will also serve to notify him of your interest in welfare.
2. Write SRS/HEW for a copy of current federal AFDC regulations as published in the Federal Register.
3. For a broader view of welfare programs see Gilbert Y. Steiner, The State of Welfare (Washington: The Brookings

Institution, 1971). Includes information on veterans' pensions, food stamps, public housing, and day care.

4. For a detailed treatment of the intergovernmental relations involved in welfare see Wayne Vasey, Government and Social Welfare: Roles of Federal, State and Local Government in Administering Welfare Services **(New York: Henry Holt and Company, 1958).**

5. For a good introduction to the whole field of social welfare see Walter A. Friedlander, Introduction to Social Welfare **(2d ed.; Englewood Cliffs, N.J.: Prentice-Hall, 1961).**

6. Find out about the administrative setup of welfare in your locality and state and fill in the blanks in the chart on page 33 by following it up the line.

7. Write your state legislator for
   a. a copy of your state's welfare law,
   b. information on how you can obtain (or at least see and use) the state welfare regulations and manual, and
   c. the latest state welfare legislative committee proposals/reports.

8. Write your state welfare department for
   a. pamphlets explaining how to get welfare and how to appeal,
   b. the latest statistics on welfare in your state.

9. VISIT your local welfare department and
   a. see how the waiting room looks and how people are treated, how long they wait, etc.,
   b. get a copy of the AFDC application form,
   c. ask how long it takes to get AFDC and whether emergency aid is given when needed in the waiting period,
   d. ask if you can look at the local and state regulations, and
   e. ask for the local statistics as to how many adults and children are on welfare, and available information about their ages, employability, etc.

10. Find out about any local welfare citizens (advisory) board. Who is on it? When and where does it meet?

11. When was the last study of welfare in your town? Has the

League of Women Voters studied welfare in your town? Is there a church group concerned with welfare? Is there a welfare rights organization? *

12. Think through the ways in which you are "on welfare." Use the checklist on pp. 40–42 as a guide. For a provocative view of government subsidies, see Leonard Baker, The Guaranteed Society (New York: Macmillan, 1968). Especially good regarding patents, SST, and oil shale.

WHAT IS WELFARE?

Proponents of a Government program designed to aid a particular industry, group, or type of enterprise avoid and indeed resent the term "subsidy" in describing their program, preferring to call it an aid or an expenditure necessary in the national interest or defense.

DEFINING A SUBSIDY

In the United States, and doubtless in other countries, there is a distaste for receiving from Government what is labeled as subsidy. There is, I hasten to add, ample willingness to take benefits from Government. But there is strong preference for forms which help conceal the nature of the receipt.

1. *Tax exemption,* for example, seems far more attractive than a governmental payment yielding the same economic benefit. The modern search for benefit often takes this form.

2. Business as well as individuals are willing to accept *commercial-type services* from Government at *less than cost.*

* Welfare has been a national priority issue of the League of Women Voters recently. The United Methodist Church and the United Church of Christ are two Protestant denominations which have been active nationally on welfare issues. Information on local Welfare Rights Organizations in your area can be obtained from the National Welfare Rights Organization, 1424—16th St. N.W., Washington, D.C. 20036.

3. A different type of example arises from the development of social insurance systems which replace programs resting on need. When benefits are set definitely by law, do we ever think of the person who gets more than he paid as receiving a subsidy? Not as a rule, I believe. As governmental expenditures have grown, they have included more of outlays which have a big element of individual benefit. General social welfare is no longer the overwhelming criterion of public spending. Is there, then, a subsidy element?

4. A fourth example arises from governmental assumption of some of the cost of borrowing money. *The Treasury's aid is not always obvious.* As a rule it is too complex to be measured. Rarely does the person who benefits sense that some of what he receives is at the expense of someone else. Yet the examples of such aid are numerous.[1]

General agreement on a definition may well, under the circumstances, be unattainable. Perhaps the best that can be done is to examine some of the numerous definitions that have been attempted.

Source: Subsidy and Subsidy-effect
Programs of the U. S. Government
Materials Prepared by The Joint
Economic Committee, Congress of the
United States, 89th Congress,
1st Session Joint Committee Print,
1965, p. 3.

ARE *YOU* ON THE WELFARE?

A Beginning Checklist:

SCOPE OF SUBSIDIES:

I. **Grants to Business Firms and Corporations to Carry Out Specific Objectives**

[1] C. Lowell Harris, "Subsidies in the United States," **Public Finance,** vol. 16, 1961: 271.

—Shipbuilding and ship operating differential subsidy
—Land grants and cash contributions for railroad construction
—Subsidies for carrying mail—civil air carriers

II. **Farm Subsidy Programs**
—Commodity price support program
—Surplus disposal programs, domestic and export
—Conservation and soil bank payments
—Irrigation and flood control
—Agricultural extension services

III. **Tax Benefits to Specific Economic Groups**
—Depletion allowances to oil and minerals producers
—Investment tax credits to modernize plants and machinery
—Tax deductions such as of mortgage interest and property taxes which benefit particular groups (homeowners vs. tenants)

IV. **Indirect Assistance to Specific Economic Groups**
—Financing of highway construction (trucking industry)
—Financing of airport construction
—Protective tariffs

V. **Government Economic Programs with Incidental Economic Effects Similar to Those of Subsidies**
—Letting of government contracts for supplies, research and development, etc.
—Disposal of surplus property at less than market value
—Stockpiling of minerals and other strategic materials

VI. **Free or Below Cost Services Offered by the Federal Government**
—Statistical information of many kinds of importance to business, industry and labor
—Scientific and industrial research
—Certain postal services provided below cost

VII. **Lending and Loan Guarantee Programs**

    —Farmers Home Administration
    —Commodity Credit loans
    —Student loans
    —Small business loans
    —Federal Housing Administration loans

VIII. **Insurance Programs Undertaken by the Federal Government**
    —Agricultural crop insurance
    —Bank deposit insurance
    —Veterans' life insurance

IX. **Federal Aid Payments to States and Local Units**
    —Accelerated public works program
    —Disaster relief
    —Urban renewal
    —Assistance for school construction

X. **Federal Aid Payments to Individuals, etc., Within the States**
    —Rural housing grants
    —Civil defense
    —National Guard
    —Public health research
    —Hospital construction
    —Manpower training

Source: Excerpted from a comprehensive annotated list in materials prepared by the Joint Economic Committee (see previous citation, p. 40), pp. 11–19.

CALIFORNIA WELFARE APPLICATION FORM

Important Notice to Public Assistance Applicants and Recipients

All of us in your County Welfare Department want you to receive assistance promptly and in the right amount, if it is determined you are eligible. Our objective is to complete the necessary investigation to determine if you are eligible at the earliest possible date and within a maximum of 30 days after the date of your application. There are sometimes factors beyond our control which may delay the investigation beyond this 30 day standard. We will try to do our part to prevent unnecessary delays. However, the period required to complete the investigation is often dependent on you. Your part is in providing us promptly with any information or evidence you have or which is readily available to you and is needed by us to assist in determining your eligibility.

You should notify us immediately if you move to another address. Otherwise, processing of your application may be delayed.

If you are found eligible to assistance, you are required to notify us when there is any change in your income, your needs, or financial circumstances. Should you fail to report the facts regarding these matters you might not receive the full amount of aid to which you are entitled. On the other hand if you fail to report promptly you may receive more aid than you are entitled to receive under the law. If you do receive aid to which you are not entitled because you failed to report the facts to us we must demand repayment from you and you may be subject to criminal prosecution.

The following statements may help you to understand the kind of facts which you are required to report.

Notify us if you buy or sell any real property, or if you sell any of your personal property.

Notify us if someone dies and leaves you some money or property, or if you receive money or property from any other source.

Notify us if you begin to receive income from earnings, relatives, social security benefits, rent from any property you may own, or income from any other source. Notify us if you begin to receive free rent in the place you live.

Even if you have already notified us that you are receiving income from some source, let us know if that income increases. You should also let us know if that income decreases or if it stops.

When there is any change in your need, your income or property holdings, or someone moves into or out of your household, notify us immediately by letter, by calling at our office, or by telephone. DO NOT DELAY until someone from our department calls on you. That may be too late.

County Welfare Department

If you have any questions or you desire further information regarding your application, including the period required to investigate your eligibility:

You may get in touch with your social worker who will be glad to discuss your problem with you. All facts and any further information you wish to present will be given careful consideration. If an adjustment is in order, it will be made.

You may inform the nearest office of the State Department of Social Welfare of your complaint by going in person, or writing to that office. The Department will then notify the county welfare department. Upon receipt of this notification the county welfare department will review the facts in your case. If they determine that you are entitled to an adjustment, it may be possible to settle your complaint without further action on your part.

You may request a fair hearing, and a decision by the Director of the State Department of Social Welfare. Such request must be in writing. A letter is sufficient but you must state that you want a hearing and tell why you are dissatisfied.

If you wish a hearing send your letter requesting such a hearing to the nearest office of the State Department of Social Welfare. A request for a hearing to be considered must be received by the State Department of Social Welfare within one year of the postmarked date of the notice of action with which you are dissatisfied.

THEY DON'T GIVE YOU A COPY OF THIS WHEN YOU APPLY—THEY OUGHT TO

THE TEN COMMANDMENTS
(For a Mother on Welfare)

1. Thou shall give your children what they need but don't spend over 75¢ a day
2. Thou shall have furniture if glue will hold it together
3. Thou shall live in a real nice house in the slums
4. Thou shall clothe thy children as long as they are rags
5. Thou shall send thy children to school but don't give them any supplies
6. Thou shall feed thy children but don't give them meat
7. Thou shall not buy any under clothes. No one sees them
8. Thou shall not give thy children spending money. Let them beg
9. Thou shall not ride a bus up-town! Walk
10. Thou shall not get sick—just die!

by Mary Magdalene Spurlock,
a mother on A.D.C.

Welfare from the Bottom Up!
"I WISH MY CASEWORKER WOULD . . ."

- "see me like a human being"
- "not 'talk down' to me"
- "take time to explain my budget to me"
- "not be so young and know something about 'how it is' "
- "know what she's talking about—one time she tells me one thing—next time another"
- "not tell me the only way I can get more money is to have another baby"
- "try to help me with my problems and my children"
- "say what she means"
- "see what she can do so my children can get shoes when they need them"

- "stop looking for a man in my house—she always acts like she thinks I have a man in there"
- "ask me why I want to take part in everything." She asked, "Do your children get on your nerves so you have to leave the house?"
- "help me to get a job"
  "be more like Mrs. Wesley, 'cause she tries to help you"
  (our Avalon-CWD Project Caseworker)
- "tell me before time when my check is going to be late"
- "stop saying she'll hold my check, if I don't do this or that"
- "come to see me when she says she's going to, so I don't have to sit around the house all day waiting for her. I've got things to do too"
- "help me with car fare and books so I can go to school myself"
- "stop acting like that money she gives me is hers"
- "would just once—explain the CWD policy and the rules and regulations so that I will know"
- "would stop comparing me and my circumstances with her and her circumstances"

by AFDC mothers in the Avalon Central
Demonstration Project of the Avalon-Carver
Community Center, Los Angeles, California—1963.

☞ CHAPTER TWO
HISTORY:
WHERE DID WELFARE COME FROM?

The idea of charity has probably been with us as long as the poor have. But the development of our "modern" system of **public** aid essentially dates from the beginnings of the Industrial Revolution. In addition to the "charitable impulse" welfare clearly developed out of concerns of the nonpoor about their **own** welfare (p. 51).*

FROM ENGLAND
As feudalism began to give way to a wage economy and serfs became free workers, problems began for both worker and society. Instead of the economic security accorded the serf by his master, the free worker faced starvation if he could not find work. Thus, as those who could not find work turned to begging (and/or crime) and as they moved about in search of work they posed a problem to the lords. When famine and plague sharply reduced the supply of available workers at the same time the economy was becoming newly dependent on wage earners, the lords turned to government to insure that begging did not become an alternative to "participating in the labor market." Thus the first poor laws were efforts to control and regulate begging (pp. 52–53).

* Page numbers in the section refer the reader to illustrative materials at the end of this chapter.

By 1601 the English Poor Law was substantially complete—and ready to be taken to the New World by the American colonists (p. 54).

A look at its principal features easily illustrates the source of our welfare ideas:

1. **Public financing** by taxing property owners (pp. 54–55).
2. **Local administration** for local **residents** only (pp. 55–57).
3. **Relatives responsible** for assistance to their relations (pp. 57–58).
4. Different **categories** of aid including, but separating, aged, sick and disabled, children, and able-bodied unemployed.
5. **Less eligibility**—always provide less aid than the lowest-paid worker's wages (p. 59).
6. **Work and workhouse test**—no aid if indigent refused work and/or refused to go to the workhouse (pp. 59–61).

THE POOR LAW IN AMERICA

And so the Poor Law came to America. For a while—until about the Revolution—it worked out fairly well. Especially with such devices as "public vendue," that is, farming out or auctioning off the poor to the lowest bidder. Welfare was not needed as much in the South because of the existence of slavery (p. 61).

As America became more settled and more industrial, problems multiplied. Soon we took the lead in reviving the English poorhouse/workhouse approach (pp. 59–61).

With the growth of the American middle class, antirelief forces found unexpected allies—the early social workers—who led the fight against outdoor (in your own home) public relief. They were greatly concerned about the bad effect on people of receiving public money and thought private "experts" (that is, themselves) were needed to decide carefully who was deserving and how best to see that relief did not "pauperize" those receiving it (pp. 61–62).

Just after the turn of the century a new idea came to the fore: mothers' (or widows') pensions. Given impetus by the first White House Children's Conference called by President Theo-

dore Roosevelt in 1909 and advocated by settlement house re-
formers like Florence Kelley and Julia Lathrop, the first state
Mothers' Pension Law was passed in 1911 in Illinois. Many
prominent social work leaders of this time opposed mothers'
pensions as simply another form of unacceptable outdoor relief or even as "socialism." But a lively "mothers' movement"
(which included the PTA!) tipped the balance and by 1931,
1,600 counties in 45 states had some mothers' aid program
even though funds and family grants were very limited.

These programs provided the experience, framework, and
background which helped bring about the inclusion of AFDC
in the Social Security Act of 1935 (pp. 63–64).

Winifred Bell, in her helpful study of AFDC in the 1940s and
'50s, sums up this period following passage of the Social
Security Act this way:

> The advent of ADC meant that the states could receive tempt-
> ing and sorely needed federal funds in exchange for at least
> a modicum of federal control, but in programs that had been
> intimately tied to local mores and values this was not an
> easy exchange.
>   In some states the problem became one of defining eligi-
> bility so that the social change potentials of federal funding
> would be minimized.*

She also details the ways in which the states used "suitable
home" policies to restrict the growth of the caseload and to in-
hibit ADC coverage of Negro and illegitimate children.

Gilbert Y. Steiner completes the history of AFDC, bringing us
right up-to-date with a blow-by-blow account of the 1960s:

> Following 25 years without high-level attention to public as-
> sistance, a decade of tinkering began in 1961. That year the
> Kennedy administration secured approval of federal financial
> assistance to states choosing to extend their ADC program

* Winifred Bell, **Aid to Dependent Children** (New York: Columbia University Press, 1965), pp. 174–75.

to cover families whose heads are unemployed but . . . even by the end of the sixties only half the states had done so.*

He describes the focus on services in the period 1962–1967 and the bursting of the services bubble with the 1967 Social Security amendments which contained a federal AFDC "freeze" and the Work Incentive Program's mandatory work provisions foreshadowing President Nixon's call in 1970 for "workfare."
And in a nutshell that is how today's AFDC welfare system came to be!

☞ DO-ITS

1. Delve into the history of welfare in your state. California, New York, New Jersey, Illinois, Indiana, Kentucky, Vermont, North Carolina, Massachusetts, Kansas, Pennsylvania, Michigan, Ohio, Rhode Island, Iowa, Montana, Missouri, Virginia are among the states with fascinating books written on their welfare history that are available in your local public FREE library!

2. For more on the English Poor Law background, from the Statute of Laborers in 1349 to the Beveridge Report of 1942, see Karl de Schweinitz, England's Road to Social Security (Philadelphia: University of Pennsylvania Press, 1943; New York: A. S. Barnes, 1961).

3. For more on the early American experience see Blanche D. Coll, Perspectives in Public Welfare, A History (Washington: U. S. Department of Health, Education, and Welfare, Social and Rehabilitation Service, 1969).

4. For a fascinating look at original documents in the history of the American Welfare system see Edith Abbott, Public Assistance: American Principles and Policies (Chicago: University of Chicago Press, 1940; reissued New York: Russell & Russell, 1966); and Sophonisba Breckinridge, Public Welfare Administration in the United States: Select

* Gilbert Y. Steiner, **The State of Welfare** (Washington: The Brookings Institution, 1971), p. 35.

Documents **(2d ed.; Chicago: University of Chicago Press, 1938).**

5. **For a revealing account of the background leading to the passage of the Social Security Act in 1935 see Hilary M. Leyendecker,** Problems and Policy in Public Assistance **(New York: Harper & Bros., 1955).**

6. **For the basic history of AFDC in the 1940s, 1950s and early 1960s see Winifred Bell,** Aid to Dependent Children **(New York: Columbia University Press, 1965).**

7. **For recent developments in AFDC see Gilbert Y. Steiner,** The State of Welfare **(Washington: The Brookings Institution, 1971), especially chapter 2, "Tireless Tinkering with Dependent Families."**

8. **For the exciting story of how poverty was discovered in the United States complete with a fascinating history of poverty and American culture see Robert H. Bremner,** From the Depths: The Discovery of Poverty in the United States **(New York: New York University Press, 1956, 1965).**

From the Impulse to Charity

The (charitable) impulse itself, in its most primitive, and perhaps most permanent, form, is deeply ingrained in our human nature, and is encountered in all the quarters of the earth. The sight of suffering calls forth, as if by direct reflex action of brain and heart, the impulse to act, to give, to share either of our goods or of our strength to the end that the evident signs of suffering may be obliterated. It is strange how little it takes, however, even in civilized man, to satisfy this original impulse, how slight the obstacle that will suffice to prevent even its crudest expression.

Source: Edwart T. Devine,
The Principles of Relief
(New York: Macmillan, 1920),
p. 177.

And to the end that the money raised only for the relief of such as are impotent and poor may not be misapplied and consumed by the idle, sturdy, and disorderly beggars; every person put upon the collection, shall upon the shoulder of the right sleeve upon the uppermost garment, wear a badge of a large roman P. together with the first letter of the name of the parish of place where he inhabits cut in red or blue cloth.

> Source: English Law 1697,
> 829 W 3c. 30,
> quoted in Richard Burn,
> **History of the Poor Law**
> (London: H. Woodall & W. Stahan, Ltd., 1764).

A LICENSE TO BEG

The first statute, in the year 1377, to be enacted in the reign of Richard II, complains that villeins and land tenants "do daily withdraw their services and customs due to their said lords" and "affirm them to be quite and utterly discharged of all manner of servage, due as well of their body as of their said tenures," and "which more in gather themselves together in great routs and agree by such confederacy that every one shall aid other to resist their lords with strong hand."

Here was material for revolt, and four years later came Wat Tyler's attempt to force by rebellion further concessions of the direction of freedom for the serfs. He failed, but the changes of which he was evidence continued. In 1388 Parliament enacted a statute—12th Richard II—which restated the problem and attempted to improve upon the messages imposed by the first and second Statutes of Laborers.

The Statute moves further toward coercion by attempting in much more specific language than before to restrict the laborer to his place of residence.

No servant nor laborer, be he man or woman, shall depart at

the end of his term out of the hundred, rape, or wapentake where he is dwelling to serve or dwell elsewhere, or by color to go from thense in pilgramage, unless he bring a letter patent containing the cause of his going, and the time of his return . . . if . . . without such letter . . . he shall be . . . put in the stocks, and kept till he hath found surety to return to his service, or to serve or labor in the town from whence he came, till he had such letter to depart for a reasonable cause.

The penalty which the 12th Richard II inflicted upon the servant or laborer traveling without letter patent, it also employed against the beggar:

Of every person that goeth begging *and is able to serve or labor* [italics added] it shall be done of him as of him that departeth out of the hundred and other places aforesaid without letter testimonial.

While this law introduces long series of attempts to control begging through punishment, it also recognizes for the first time the possible existence of need requiring relief. The Statutes of Laborers treated the beggar, the transient, and the bargainer for high wages as problems relating to the supply of labor. The 12th Richard II, 1388, grants the plight of the unemployable and by implication approves begging as an appropriate way by which they may obtain support.

That the beggars *impotent to serve* [italics added] shall abide in the cities and towns where they be dwelling at the time of the proclamation of this statute; and if the people of cities or other towns will not or may not suffice to find them, that then the said beggars shall draw them to other towns within the hundreds, rape or wapentake, or to the towns where they were born, within forty days after the proclamation made, and there shall continually abide during their lives.

Source: Karl de Schweinitz,
England's Road to Social Security
(Philadelphia: University
of Pennsylvania Press, 1943).
Used by permission.

FROM ENGLAND

By the time of the establishment of the colonies in America, then, England had developed a system of poor relief and a code of laws defining the principles of this system which were to remain in effect in that country without fundamental change until the second quarter of the nineteenth century, and in North Carolina until the twentieth. Beginning with the purpose of suppressing begging, of making each community in some measure responsible for its own poor, and of keeping the laborer subservient to the propertied class, the English advanced slowly to the more definite recognition of the claims upon the community of the impotent poor; to the relief of this class through voluntary contributions under the supervision of the church; to the recognition of the fact that the able bodied poor may not always be able to find work; to the recognition of the dependent child as a peculiar social problem and the attempt to solve that problem by the apprenticeship system; to a consideration of the problem of the illegitimate child, with the emphasis here, it is true, on the protection of the public from the expense of the support of the child; to the definite establishment of the responsibility of each community for the care of its own poor; to the establishment of the principle that the care of the poor is a social problem to be solved by taxation. But the English had never fully divested themselves of the idea that poverty is culpable or at least that society must be protected against the designing poor. Always in the background loomed the workhouse.

> Source: Roy M. Brown, *Public Poor Relief in North Carolina* (Chapel Hill: University of North Carolina Press, 1928), p. 9. Used by permission.

FROM ALMS TO TAXES

During the reign of Edward VI and of Elizabeth there was a rapid development of the principle that the poor should be supported by taxation. The method of collecting alms for the support of the poor was revised to provide that persons appointed by the officials of the town and by the church to collect alms should on a particular Sunday "gently ask and demand of every man and woman what they of their charity would give weekly toward the relief of the poor." If any one able to give refused to do so, he was first to be "gently exhorted" by the parson and church wardens; then, if he still refused, he was to be "persuaded" by the bishop. The system of voluntary contributions probably failed, even with the persuasion of the bishop, to yield adequate funds. At any rate, we find it provided, in 1563, that if any person after being "gently exhorted" by the parson and "persuaded" by the bishop, should "obstinately refuse" to contribute to the poor fund, the bishop should have authority to require a bond of ten pounds for his appearance "at the next sessions" when the justices, if the offender remained obstinate, might in their discretion assess against him the amount which he must pay under penalty of imprisonment. Finally, in 1572, we reach the full recognition of the principle that the poor should be supported by means of a tax levied by the justices of the peace, the funds to be administered by overseers of the poor, who themselves were appointed by the justices of the peace.

Source: Roy M. Brown, *Public Poor Relief in North Carolina* (Chapel Hill: University of North Carolina Press, 1928), pp. 5–6. Used by permission.

BECAUSE LOCAL GOVERNMENT WAS RESPONSIBLE FOR ITS OWN POOR IT HAD TO:

"WARN" THEM OUT

In 1650 the General Court of the Bay passed an order which is the unmistakable forerunner of the Massachusetts law of settlement: for the avoyding of all future inconvenjencjes referring to the settling of poore people that may neede releife from the place where they dwell, it is ordered by this court and the authoritje thereof, that where any person wth his family, or in case he hath no family, shall be resident in any towne or peculiar of this jurisdiccon for more than three months without notice given to such person or persons by the constable or one of the selectmen of the sajd place, or theire order, that the towne is not willing that they should remajne as an inhabitant amongst them, and in case, after such notice given, such person or persons shall not wth standing remajne in the sajd place, if the selectmen of the sajd place shall not, by way of complaint, petition the next County Court of that shiere, every such person or persons (as the case may require) shall be provided for and releived, in case of necessity, by the inhabitants of the sajd place where he or she is so found.[1]

When the Massachusetts, Plymouth, and Connecticut colonies were consolidated under the Articles of Confederation of 1672, an express provision (article 13) was retained, establishing the three months' rule of inhabitancy and declaring the towns liable to support if they failed to warn out, or, if having warned, and the stranger having failed to go, the town did not take the first opportunity to remove him to his rightful place of abode.[2]

[1] Records of Massachusetts Bay, vol. iv, part 1.
[2] Articles of Confederation, art. 18, Sept. 3, 1672, Hazard, vol. 11, p. 595.

Source: Robert W. Kelso, *The History of Public Poor Relief in Massachusetts 1620–1920*
(Boston: Houghton Mifflin, 1922),
p. 53.

KEEP THEM OUT

Bringing pauper into county—Penalty. 13. If any person shall bring and leave any pauper in any county in this state, wherein such pauper is not lawfully settled, knowing him to be a pauper, he shall forefeit and pay the sum of $100 for every such offense, to be sued

WHERE DID WELFARE COME FROM?

for and recovered by and to the use of such county by action of debt, before any justice of the peace in the proper county. (R.S. 1845, p. 404, sec. 16)

REMOVE THEM

Removal of pauper non-resident—charges. 16. If any person shall become chargeable as a pauper in any city, village or incorporated town or county who did not reside therein at the commencement of twelve months immediately preceding his becoming so chargeable, but did at that time reside in some other city, village or incorporated town in this state charged with the relief and support of poor and indigent persons, it shall be the duty of the municipal, county or town clerk, as the case may be, to send written notice by mail or otherwise, to the clerk of such other city, village or incorporated town or county in which the pauper so resided, requesting the proper authorities of such city, village or incorporated town, county or town, as the case may be, to remove said pauper forthwith, and to pay the expenses accrued or to accrue in taking care of the same.

OR BILL ANOTHER LOCAL GOVERNMENT

Source: From Illinois Pauper and Poor Relief Laws, 1919, 1937, quoted in Edith Abbott, *Public Assistance: American Principles and Policies* (Chicago: University of Chicago Press, 1940; reissued New York: Russell & Russell, 1966), vol. I, 39, 41.

Are You a Responsible Relative?

Who first called on city, village, or incorporated town; County or town can sue relatives. 2. The children shall first be called on to support their parents, if there be children of sufficient ability; and if there be none of sufficient ability, the parents of such poor person shall next be called on if they be of sufficient ability; and if there be no parents or children of sufficient ability, the brothers and sisters of such poor person shall next be called on, if they be of sufficient ability; and if there be no brothers or sisters of sufficient ability the grandchildren of such poor person shall next be called on, if they be of sufficient ability; and next the grandparents, if they be of sufficient ability.

CONTRIBUTE

Contribution. 7. If it shall appear that the relatives of a certain degree are unable wholly to maintain such poor person, but are able to contribute towards his support, the court may, in its discretion, direct two or more relatives of different degrees to maintain such poor person, and shall prescribe the proportion which each shall contribute for that purpose.

SOMETHING

Partial support. 8. If it shall appear that the relatives liable, as aforesaid, are not of sufficient ability wholly to maintain such poor person, but are able to contribute something, the court shall direct the sum, in proportion to their ability, which such relatives shall pay weekly for that purpose.

OR ELSE

How payments enforced. 11. Payment of the several sums under such order as they fall due may be compelled by attachment as for contempt against the persons of the defendants, or by execution against their lands and tenements, goods and chattels, or both, in like manner as other judgments at law or decrees in chancery.

Source: From Illinois Pauper and Poor Relief Laws, 1919, 1937, quoted in Edith Abbott, *Public Assistance: American Principles and Policies* (Chicago: University of Chicago Press, 1940; reissued New York: Russell & Russell, 1966), Vol. I.

LESS THAN THE LOWEST PAID WORKER

The first and most essential of all conditions, a principle which we find universally admitted, even by those whose practice is at variance with it, is that his situation on the whole shall not be made really or apparently so eligible as the situation of the independent laborer of the lowest class. Throughout the evidence it is shown, that in proportion as the condition of any pauper class is elevated above the condition of independent laborers, the condition of the independent class is depressed; their industry is impaired, their employment becomes unsteady, and its remuneration in wages is diminished. Such persons, therefore, are under the strongest inducements to quit the less eligible class of laborers and enter the more eligible class of paupers. The converse is the effect when the pauper class is placed in its proper position, below the condition of the independent laborer. Every penny bestowed, that tends to render the condition of the pauper more eligible than that of the independent laborer, is a bounty on indolence and vice.

Source: Report of 1834 Poor Law Commission, England, quoted in
Roy M. Lubove, ed., *Social Welfare in Transition:*
Selected English Documents,
1834–1909 (Pittsburgh: University of Pittsburgh Press, 1966),
p. 53.

HERE IS HOW THE WORKHOUSE TEST WORKED

Rumford, Essex

The advantage of the workhouse to the parish does not arise from what the poor people can do towards their subsistence, but from the apprehensions the poor have of it. These prompt them to exert, and do their utmost to keep themselves off the parish, and render them exceedingly adverse to submit to come into the house, till extreme necessity compels them. Pride, though it does ill become poor folks, won't suffer some to wear the badge; others cannot brook confinement; and a third sort deem the workhouse to be a mere state of slavery, and so numbers are kept out.

Or Did It?

Sir Frederic Eden in his State of the Poor studies the cost in taxes in sixteen of the parishes which reported initial savings, including St. Andrew's, Holborn; Bristol; and Maidstone. He shows in each case the rate before the workhouse was started, the reduction at the time the workhouse opened, the net expenses for the poor in 1776, and the assessments in 1783, 1784, and 1785. In all except one parish, costs had mounted far above the rise in the cost of living which began in the third quarter of the eighteenth century. In St. Andrew's, for example, the taxes had doubled, and in Maidstone they had trebled.

It will appear [Sir Frederic comments] that the charge of maintaining their poor has advanced very rapidly, notwithstanding the aid of workhouses, and perhaps as rapidly as in those parishes which have continued to relieve the poor by occasional pensions at their own habitations.

Source: Karl de Schweinitz, *England's Road to Social Security* (Philadelphia: University of Pennsylvania Press, 1943). Used by permission.

WHO WAS IT FOR?

. . . all vagabonds and idle persons going about in town or country begging or persons using any subtil craft, juggling or unlawful games or plays or feigning themselves to have knowledge on physiognomy, palmistry or pretending they can tell destinies, fortunes or discover where lost goods may be found, common pipers, fiddlers, runaways, stubborn servants or children, common drunkards, common night-walkers, pilferers, wanton and lascivious persons either in speech or behavior, common railers or brawlers such as neglect their callings, misspend what they earn, and do not provide for themselves or the support of their families . . . as also persons under distraction and unfit to go at large, whose friends do not care for their safe confinement.

Source: Connecticut law, quoted in Hilary M. Leyendecker, *Problems and Policy in Public Assistance* (New York: Harper & Bros., 1955), pp. 35–36.

There Is Also a History of Involvement of the "Private Sector" in Welfare . . .

Sec. 3. That it shall be the duty of the overseers of the poor in each and every township, yearly and every year, to cause all poor persons who have, or shall become a public charge, to be farmed out at public vendue, or outcry, to wit: On the first Monday in May, yearly and every year, at some public place in each township in the several counties in this state, respectively to the person or persons, who shall appear to be the lowest bidder or bidders, having given ten days previous notice of such sale, in at least three of the most public places in their respective townships; which notices shall set forth the name and age as near as may be, of each person to be farmed out as aforesaid.

Source: Illinois Poor Law 1819, quoted in Sophonisba Breckinridge, **The Illinois Poor Law and Its Administration,** (Chicago: University of Chicago Press, 1939), pp. 243–44.

HOW TO PROVE STARVATION IS IMMINENT?

It is good for the community that no one should be allowed to starve; therefore, it is a legitimate thing that the public money should be used to prevent such a possibility, and this justifies the giving of public relief in extreme cases of distress, when starvation is imminent. Where, however, shall be found the proof that starvation is imminent? Only by putting such conditions upon the giving of public relief that, presumably, persons not in danger of starvation will not consent to receive it. The less that is given, the better for everyone, the giver and the receiver; and therefore, the conditions must be hard, although never degrading. On the contrary, they must be elevating, and this is by no means incompatible with severity . . .

A SOCIAL WORKER SPEAKS SINCERELY

Source: Josephine Shaw Lowell,
*The Economics and Moral
Effect of Public Outdoor Relief,*
quoted in Muriel W. and Ralph E. Pumphrey,
The Heritage of American Social Work
(New York: Columbia University Press, 1961),
p. 223.

History of Welfare in America from 1600 to 1930: A Quick Summary

The pattern of poor relief based upon the English poor law survived almost unchanged from the colonial period until the present era. It is astonishing that in spite of political, economic, and social changes that took place during that period an institution presumably geared to the needs of the people could have shown so little development. But perhaps it was because the attention and energy of the American people were focused on progress in so many other areas that they had little time to consider the problem of human wastage and misery.

Because of the prevailing opinion that poverty was usually the result of one's personal shortcomings, little effort was made to understand its causes and the need for variation in treatment.

Source: Hilary M. Leyendecker, *Problems and
Policy in Public Assistance*
(New York: Harper & Bros., 1955), p. 36.

WHERE DID WELFARE COME FROM?

MOTHERS' PENSIONS—
A BETTER NAME THAN AFDC?

Illinois led the way with its "Funds to Parents" Act: that important year, 1911, the legislature of Missouri authorized Jackson County (Kansas City) to provide Mothers' pensions. . . .

The storm of controversy that developed among social workers with the passage of the Illinois Act showed how out of line many of them were with current public opinion and how little they appreciated the needs of mothers who were not cared for or were very inadequately cared for by the private charity they administered. The Illinois law was proposed by Judge Merritt W. Pinckney, of the Cook County Juvenile Court because he found himself continually asked to take children from poor but competent mothers and commit them to institutions. Public relief in Cook County was at that time limited to grocery and coal orders which the United Charities and other private agencies often supplemented by money for rent, clothes, and types of food not supplied by the County. But such assistance was generally regarded as emergency aid. Usually work was secured for the mother, and sometimes she was persuaded to give up one or two children when it was obvious that she could not hope even with some assistance combined with her meager earnings to care for all her children. At the White House Conference on Dependent Children which President Theodore Roosevelt called in 1909, the first resolution adopted laid great stress on the importance of providing means for keeping children in their own homes. . . .

In two years twenty states, in ten years forty states, and by 1935 all the states except Georgia and South Carolina had passed some kind of mothers' aid laws.

The rapid enactment of mothers' aid constituted public recognition by the states that the contribution of the unskilled or semiskilled mothers in their own homes exceeded their earnings outside of the home, that it was in the public interest to conserve their child-caring functions, and as this group of children whose fathers were dead, incapacitated, or had deserted them would need care for a long period, the states recognized that the aid should not be administered in connection with or as part of general relief and must have a standard of adequacy from that of emergency relief. This legislation also represented a revolt against the current policy of separating children from their mothers on the ground of poverty alone and caring for them at greater cost in institutions and in foster homes.

Source: Grace Abbott, *From Relief to Social Security* (Chicago: University of Chicago Press, 1941), pp. 262–65.

THE DEBATE

SOCIAL WORK'S "FOUNDING MOTHER" MARY RICHMOND

WRONG

So far from being a forward step, "funds to parents" is a backward one—public funds not to widows only, mark you, but to private families, funds to the families of those who have deserted and are going to desert! . . . No private fund for relief can successfully compete very long with a public fund, whether the latter is adequate or not. Inevitably the sources of private charitable relief dry up!

Source: Grace Abbott, ed., *The Child and State* (Chicago: University of Chicago Press), p. 232.

AT FIRST THEY WERE ILLEGAL!

Under the title "A Grim Absurdity in the New York City Charter," the report described a situation that existed until recent years in a number of localities in other states, by legal limitation of public relief, or in practice: "By a legal restriction the Commissioner of Charities of New York City may board dependent children with other families but may not do so in their own families regardless of the worthiness of the parents. In other words, he may pay Mrs. Brown for caring for the children of Mrs. Jones, whom he may in turn compensate for the care of Mrs. Brown's children. Here at last we have the final absurdity to which our present system of separating families because of poverty is reducible."

GOD vs. "The Charitable People"

Check out how much foster parents are paid vs. AFDC grants today!

An illustration of this system was supplied by Mrs. Florence Kelley, head of the National Consumers' League:

There was a man who was a teamster, taking perfectly good care of his wife and six children. He was thrown from his team and killed. Three of his children were taken from their mother and put in an institution, and then were taken from the institution and given to somebody else to take care of who was paid out of the city funds for taking care of them. A neighbor of the man, talking to me about this expressed himself with considerable bitterness. He said, "God evidently thought that woman was able to take care of her children till Tim fell off the seat of his wagon; but the charitable people knew better and thought the children could not be taken proper care of by their mother, but had to be given to another widow to enable her to eke out her living."

Source: Emma Lundberg, *Unto the Least of These, Social Services for Children* (New York: Appleton-Century-Crofts, 1947). Used by permission of Clarence E. McDermaid.

Homer Folks, secretary of the New York State Charities Aid Association, took a different position. He said that while there was a subtle psychological but very important difference between the feeling of reliance upon private relief and the feeling of reliance upon public charity, claimed as a matter of right, I am not so sure, in the case of widows, that it is not a matter of right after all. A feeling of reliance upon a steady and regular income wisely adapted to the family needs and the family budget, ought to be a good thing. . . . If it develops that sufficient private resources are not to be had, is the evil of breaking up families as we are now doing, a lesser evil than public relief to widows? A good many say yes. My opinion is distinctly not, and that if we do not secure from private sources sufficient funds, then, without hesitation we ought to have a system of public relief for widows.

RIGHT

Source: Grace Abbott, ed., *The Child and State*
(Chicago: University of Chicago Press), p. 233.

WHERE DID WELFARE COME FROM?

☞ CHAPTER THREE
THE FACTS
ABOUT WELFARE

Now let us look at the basic facts about welfare. Our effort here will be to let the facts speak for themselves. Try the accompanying charts and tables if the written-out facts bog you down and vice versa.

The facts presented are organized around the following questions.

- How many people receive welfare?
- Where do the people on welfare live?
- Who are the people on AFDC and why are they on welfare?
- How much money do the families on welfare get and where does it come from?
- What other aid do welfare recipients get?
- How many people are poor?
- How does what we spend on welfare compare with . . . the federal budget, state and local budgets?
- What are the facts about work? about illegitimacy?
- Why are the welfare rolls rising?
- What are the facts about old people on welfare?

It must be emphasized that the material has been selected from the **most recently available** government studies and statistics. This means that not all the data are from the same year, and in some instances a listing may have figures from more than one year. But these variations are identified.

HOW MANY PEOPLE RECEIVE WELFARE?

As of January 1972 almost 15 million people were receiving welfare in the United States.

Of the 15 million 10.7 million were parents and children receiving AFDC.

This included 2.9 million families made up of 7.7 million children and 3 million adults.

AFDC thus accounted for 72% of all welfare recipients.

There were also 2 million old people (13%) and 1.1 million blind and disabled people (7 + %) on welfare.

General assistance to single people and families not eligible for AFDC accounted for one million additional welfare recipients (7 + %).

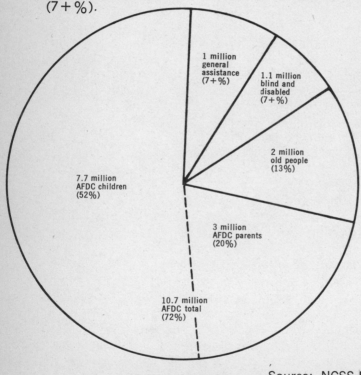

1 million general assistance (7 + %)

1.1 million blind and disabled (7 + %)

2 million old people (13%)

7.7 million AFDC children (52%)

3 million AFDC parents (20%)

10.7 million AFDC total (72%)

15 MILLION PEOPLE   Source: NCSS Report A-2, Jan. 1972.

THE FACTS ABOUT WELFARE

In terms of cost, AFDC represented about 62%, Old Age Assistance about 18%, Aid to the Blind and Aid to the Permanently and Totally Disabled about 13% and General Assistance about 7% of the total money payments for public assistance in January 1972.

There are about 204 million Americans (as of the 1970 census) so the 15 million persons on welfare are about 7 + % of us or about one out of every 14 Americans.

WHERE DO THE PEOPLE ON WELFARE LIVE?

Of the 2.9 million families receiving AFDC 1.6 million (about 55%) live in the 9 states (outside the South) with the most population: California, New York, Illinois, Pennsylvania, Ohio, Michigan, New Jersey, Massachusetts, and Indiana. Of these almost half—795,000 families—live in California and New York. (This represents over one fourth of the **national** total!)

695,000 families (24%) live in the South: Alabama, Arkansas, District of Columbia, Florida, Georgia, Louisiana, Maryland, Mississippi, North Carolina, South Carolina, Tennessee, Texas, and Virginia. (Source: NCSS Report A-2, Jan. 1972.)

More than 70% of AFDC recipients live in urban areas and 56% of all AFDC recipients live in the central city. Thirty percent live in rural areas.

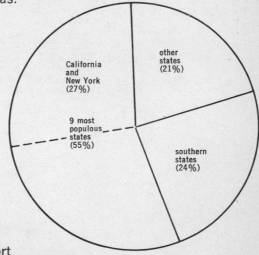

California
and
New York
(27%)

other
states
(21%)

9 most
populous
states
(55%)

southern
states
(24%)

Source: NCSS Report
AFDC-2, 1971.   WHERE AFDC FAMILIES LIVE   69

AFDC RECIPIENTS BY STATES[1]

State	Number of families	Number of recipients Total (2)	Number of recipients Children	State	Number of families	Number of recipients Total (2)	Number of recipients Children
Total (3)	2,934,924	10,695,556	7,732,378	Mont......	6,160	20,029	14,884
				Nebr. (3)..	11,803	41,333	30,462
Ala........	40,841	148,795	113,051	Nev.......	4,315	15,104	11,177
Alaska....	3,602	10,873	8,144				
Ariz.......	17,910	67,201	51,624	N.H.......	5,479	18,519	13,343
Ark.......	20,627	74,150	55,452	N.J. (4)...	102,000	374,000	270,000
Calif. (3)..	443,905	1,518,211	1,058,968	N. Mex....	15,636	56,033	42,353
Colo. (3)...	29,623	102,982	73,809	N.Y. (3)...	350,573	1,283,926	908,496
Conn......	30,950	109,370	81,893	N.C.......	46,147	167,049	125,016
Del. (3)...	8,687	30,931	22,513	N. Dak....	4,092	13,969	10,387
D.C. (3)...	24,681	87,546	64,416	Ohio (3)...	120,645	441,425	318,402
Fla........	85,961	313,084	238,599	Okla. (3)..	31,749	113,941	84,919
				Oreg. (3)..	27,328	94,790	63,924
Ga........	91,380	312,189	231,627	Pa. (3)....	172,841	664,946	460,872
Guam.....	594	2,676	2,121				
Hawaii (3).	10,761	38,919	27,026	P.R.......	52,617	266,158	192,494
Idaho.....	6,263	21,176	14,883	R.I. (3)....	13,703	50,442	35,809
Ill. (3)....	173,156	686,325	499,504	S.C.......	23,892	91,811	69,063
Ind.......	43,933	158,184	116,777	S. Dak.....	5,770	20,014	14,869
Iowa......	23,440	82,036	58,028	Tenn......	54,177	188,882	143,163
Kans. (3)..	20,957	72,792	54,551	Tex.......	110,586	423,764	313,676
Ky........	39,692	142,476	101,729	Utah (3)...	12,072	43,763	29,907
La........	60,977	241,250	185,998	Vt. (3)....	4,871	17,410	12,120
				V.I........	740	2,931	2,427
Maine (3)..	17,339	61,880	44,189	Va........	40,707	146,970	107,752
Md. (3)...	53,246	192,964	143,187				
Mass. (3)..	80,128	283,714	204,218	Wash. (3)..	44,395	150,131	99,800
Mich. (3)..	144,618	520,938	375,569	W. Va. (3).	21,895	85,954	60,830
Minn. (3)..	36,709	118,904	86,830	Wis. (3)...	36,531	(4) 128,676	(4) 94,248
Miss......	41,256	154,956	123,273	Wyo.......	2,112	7,178	5,357
Mo........	60,852	211,886	158,649				

(1) All data subject to revision. Data also include AFDC-foster care; separate data for foster care appear in releases for February, May, August, and November.

(2) Includes as recipients the children and 1 or both parents or 1 caretaker relative other than a parent in families in which the requirements of such adults were considered in determining the amount of assistance.

(3) Includes data on unemployed-parent segment.

(4) Estimated by State.

Source: NCSS Report A-2,
Jan. 1972.

THE FACTS ABOUT WELFARE

WHO ARE THE PEOPLE ON AFDC AND WHY ARE THEY ON WELFARE?

- Forty-eight percent of AFDC recipients were white, 43% were black.
- Fifty-four percent of the AFDC families had only one or two children. The median number of children per family was 2.8.

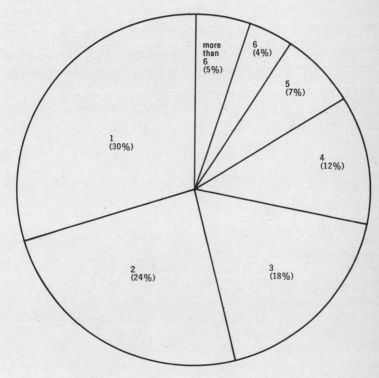

NUMBER OF CHILDREN PER AFDC FAMILY

Source: NCSS Report AFDC 2, 3, 4, 1971.

- Seventy-one percent of the children receiving AFDC were in families where all the children had the same mother and father.
- In 81% of AFDC families the father was absent from the home. The father was in the home but unemployed or incapacitated in 19% of the families.
- In 14% of AFDC families the mother was employed full or part time. And in 6% more the mother was enrolled in a work or training program (or accepted and awaiting enrollment). In addition, 5% of AFDC mothers were actively seeking work.
- Of all AFDC families in 1971 68% were on AFDC for the first time. **The average length of time they had received AFDC was less than 2 years and only 6% of the families had been on welfare more than 10 years.** (Source: NCSS Report AFDC-1, 1971; [SRS 72-03756].)

Examples of the reasons for families getting on welfare include loss of income due to illness of a parent or loss of job by a parent, father leaving home, change in the law, increased need (such as medical expense).

HOW MUCH MONEY DO THE FAMILIES ON WELFARE GET AND WHERE DOES IT COME FROM?

For the fiscal year ended June 30, 1970, AFDC families received a total of about $4 billion.

Of this amount $2.2 billion (54%) came from federal funds, $1.4 billion (35%) came from state funds, and $400 million (11%) from local funds.

It cost almost $900 million additional for administration, services, and training related to AFDC. The federal government paid 65% of this with the states putting up 21% and local government 14%. This meant a total of almost $5 billion spent on AFDC, of which administration and services costs totaled nearly 17%. (Source: NCSS Reports F-1, 2, 3, Fiscal Year 1970.)

On the following chart, see how welfare costs were shared in your state.

WHERE DOES THE MONEY YOUR STATE SPENDS ON AFDC COME FROM?

EXPENDITURES FOR AFDC AND PERCENTAGE FROM FEDERAL GOVERNMENT, FISCAL YEAR 1970

State	Amount in Millions	% Federal Funds	% State Funds	% Local Funds
Alabama.............	29	77.0	22.6	.4
Alaska..............	6	57.4	42.6	...
Arizona.............	24	74.5	24.9	.6
Arkansas...........	15	77.6	22.4	...
California..........	918	52.3	26.4	21.2
Colorado...........	41	58.0	22.5	19.5
Connecticut........	77	45.4	54.6	...
Delaware...........	9	63.7	36.3	...
Dist. of Columbia....	31	53.7	46.3	...
Florida.............	69	76.0	24.0	...
Georgia.............	78	75.0	20.6	4.3
Guam..............	1	50.5	49.5	...
Hawaii.............	19	50.6	49.4	...
Idaho..............	11	68.5	31.2	.2
Illinois.............	270	45.9	54.1	...
Indiana.............	40	58.9	24.8	16.3
Iowa...............	45	56.2	24.2	19.6
Kansas.............	39	58.5	22.2	19.4
Kentucky...........	53	74.2	25.8	...
Louisiana...........	62	77.1	22.9	...
Maine..............	22	70.0	20.6	9.4
Maryland...........	85	58.2	38.0	3.8
Massachusetts......	188	46.9	53.1	(1)
Michigan...........	195	52.2	47.6	.2
Minnesota..........	73	58.6	19.0	22.5
Mississippi.........	20	79.1	20.3	.6
Missouri............	64	71.4	28.5	.1
Montana...........	9	64.5	21.9	13.6
Nebraska...........	18	61.9	38.1	(1)
Nevada.............	7	67.0	33.0	...
New Hampshire.....	6	61.3	38.7	...
New Jersey.........	242	41.6	41.1	17.3
New Mexico........	25	74.9	25.1	...
New York...........	1,002	50.9	24.8	24.3
North Carolina......	56	71.8	15.5	12.7
North Dakota.......	9	69.6	21.7	8.7
Ohio...............	141	56.8	39.6	3.6
Oklahoma..........	54	66.8	33.2	...
Oregon.............	52	59.5	40.5	...

(1) Less than 0.05%.

State	Amount in Millions	% Federal Funds	% State Funds	% Local Funds
Pennsylvania........	329	55.2	44.8	...
Puerto Rico..........	33	48.1	51.9	...
Rhode Island........	27	50.1	49.9	...
South Carolina......	16	76.6	22.1	1.3
South Dakota........	10	65.3	34.3	.4
Tennessee..........	56	74.4	21.2	4.4
Texas.................	86	74.9	25.0	.1
Utah.................	20	69.2	30.8	(1)
Vermont.............	9	65.7	34.3	...
Virgin Islands........	1	49.1	50.9	...
Virginia..............	52	64.7	18.8	16.5
Washington.........	102	55.7	44.3	...
West Virginia........	41	75.6	24.4	...
Wisconsin...........	68	59.8	22.1	18.1
Wyoming............	4	60.5	18.1	21.4

Source: NCSS Report F-2,
Fiscal Year
1970.

A total of 177,000 persons were employed to administer welfare (as of June 1970) and AFDC accounted for 56% of them. (Source: NCSS Report E-2, Fiscal Year 1970.)

The average money payment per AFDC recipient as of January 1972 was $51.97 per month.

The highest grant was in New York which paid $79.98 per recipient per month compared with the lowest in Mississippi which paid $14.73 per recipient per month.

States with the highest payments included Alaska, Connecticut, Hawaii, Massachusetts, Michigan, Minnesota, New York, New Jersey, Vermont, Wisconsin—all over $65 per recipient per month.

States with the lowest grants included Alabama, Florida, Louisiana, Mississippi, South Carolina—all below $25 per recipient per month.

For a family of four (mother and three children) this works out to a current national average AFDC grant of $197 per month (or about $2,400 **per year.**) The average income for an AFDC family of four **including income from other than assistance** (only

THE FACTS ABOUT WELFARE

40% of all AFDC families have any such additional income) was $232 per month or about $2,800 a year.

Besides looking at the average amount of welfare paid to each recipient another important fact is how much each state recognizes that a family needs **and** how much of that need the state will meet if the family has no other income.

The **need** recognized by each state ranges from $400 per month in Alaska and $363 per month in Indiana to North Carolina which says a family of four needs only $184 per month.

However, states which recognize **more** need may **pay** less. For example, Indiana pays only 57% of its standard of need. Mississippi and Louisiana, neighboring states, differ in that Mississippi says a family of four **needs** $277 per month but pays only 22% of that (about $60 per month), while Louisiana sets need at less ($204 per month) but pays more (51% or about $104 per month).

It is important to understand these three **different** ways of looking at welfare payments: (1) the **standard** is the amount each state determines is the minimum amount needed by a family with no other income; (2) the **maximum** is the largest amount the state pays to such a family (may be a fixed dollar limit or a percentage); and (3) the **average grant** based on the actual payments to all families. Since 60 percent of AFDC families have no income except welfare, average grant figures (which include lower grants paid to families with some non-welfare income) somewhat understate grant levels. Example: District of Columbia standard is $318 per month, maximum is $239, and average is $199. (Note: the average payment also must be adjusted slightly to be comparable for a family of four since average AFDC family is slightly less than four.)

WE SAY THEY *NEED*—BUT ONLY *PAY:*

Aid to Families with Dependent Children: Full monthly standard for basic needs for a family consisting of four recipients, largest amount that can be paid to such a family, and average grant by state

State	Full Standard	Largest Amount Paid	Payments to Recipients Average Grant per Family	Average Grant per Recipient
Ala.	$232	$ 81	$ 58.99	$16.19
Alaska	400	372	217.50	72.05
Ariz.	256	167	119.24	31.78
Ark.	229	111	96.57	26.86
Calif.	274	261	204.10	59.68
Colo.	242	242	177.59	51.08
Conn.	327	327	234.01	66.22
Del.	287	172	122.21	34.32
D.C.	318	239	198.75	56.03
Fla.	223	134	90.31	24.80
Ga.	227	149	101.06	29.58
Guam	(1)	(1)	208.31	46.24
Hawaii	271	271	274.19	75.81
Idaho	272	241	202.67	59.94
Ill.	272	272	235.07	59.31
Ind.	363	205	151.97	42.21
Iowa	300	243	189.28	54.08
Kansas	335	321	168.46	48.50
Ky.	234	171	118.69	33.07
La.	204	104	87.94	22.23
Maine	349	168	141.14	39.55
Md.	311	200	160.01	44.15
Mass.	349	349	246.38	69.58
Mich.	350	350	237.72	65.99
Minn.	334	334	234.93	72.53
Miss.	277	60	55.34	14.73
Mo.	303	130	108.30	31.10
Mont.	225	206	152.48	46.90
Neb.	347	226	151.51	43.26
Nev.	320	176	119.82	34.23
N.H.	294	294	216.03	63.91
N.J.	(2) 324	(2) 324	265.69	72.46
N. Mex.	203	179	115.40	32.20
N.Y.	336	313	292.91	79.98
N.C.	184	159	117.18	32.37
N.D.	(2) 300	(2) 300	202.65	59.36
Ohio	258	200	160.54	43.88
Okla.	222	189	139.28	38.81
Ore.	349	279	176.09	50.77
Pa.	313	313	238.32	61.95
P.R.	132	53	46.50	9.19
R.I.	263	263	222.99	60.58

(1) Data not reported.
(2) Flat allowance; includes special needs.

THE FACTS ABOUT WELFARE

State	Full Standard	Largest Amount Paid	Payments to Recipients Average Grant per Family	Average Grant per Recipient
S.C..................	198	103	76.38	19.88
S.D..................	300	270	160.48	46.26
Tenn................	217	129	104.16	29.88
Texas...............	197	148	115.92	30.25
Utah................	320	218	183.70	50.67
Vt...................	327	327	232.94	65.17
V.I..................	166	166	136.70	34.51
Va..................	279	261	173.71	48.11
Wash...............	286	274	200.71	59.35
W. Va...............	265	138	116.74	29.74
Wis.................	303	274	248.30	70.49
Wyo................	283	227	146.65	43.15

Sources: Monthly standard and largest amount paid:
NCSS Report D-2 (SRS 72-03200), July 1971.
Average grants data:
NCSS Report A-2, Jan. 1972.

WHAT OTHER AID DO WELFARE RECIPIENTS GET?
AFDC recipients also may receive other aid such as food stamps or commodities, medical care, public housing, day care or other social services and may also have some other income from earnings, Social Security, child support payments, unemployment compensation, etc. As already noted, 40 percent of AFDC families had income from some source other than welfare. The remainder, however, had no other income.

Food Stamps and Commodities
Seventy-eight percent of all AFDC families in 1971 lived in areas which had a food stamp program and a total of 53 percent of AFDC families participated in this program.

Another 15 percent of AFDC families received surplus commodities. These food programs added an estimated equivalent of about $400-$500 a year to family income. (Source: Family Assistance Act of 1970, Hearings Before Senate Finance Committee, 91st Congress Second Session, Part 1, p. 374, and NCSS Report AFDC-1, 1971.) **Note:** Families with **any** outside income receive less benefit from these food programs.

Medical Care

AFDC recipients may receive medical care under Title 19 of the Social Security Act (the Medicaid Program) or through public assistance medical care arrangements authorized prior to Medicaid. This in 1969 was estimated to cost between $400 and $1,200 per year per family (varying widely from state to state). Payments were made in behalf of about 31 percent of all AFDC recipients as of May 1971. (Sources: Senate Hearings cited above, and NCSS Report B-1, May 1971.)

Public Housing

In 1967 about 12 percent of AFDC families lived in public housing projects. The amount of housing subsidy provided, that is, value of housing not paid by rent, was estimated at about $50 per month for these families. (Source: NCSS Report AFDC-2, 1969, and Gilbert Y. Steiner, **The State of Welfare** [Washington: The Brookings Institution, 1971], p. 122.)

Social Security

153,000 families (nearly 6 percent of all AFDC families) in 1971 also received some Social Security benefits (usually because of the father's death or disability). The average supplementary amount received by these families from this source was $118 a month. (Source: NCSS Report, AFDC-2, 1971 [SRS 72-03757].)

Outside Income

We repeat that only 40 percent of all AFDC families had income from any source other than welfare. For these families outside income averaged about $159 per month (about $1,900 per year). **Note:** This also varies widely from state to state. (Source: NCSS Report, AFDC-2, 1971, table 56.)

The most usual sources of such income were: earnings of family members (including those of children) 17%, support from absent fathers 13%, Social Security benefits 6%, and unemployment compensation 1%.

HOW MANY PEOPLE ARE POOR?

Now that we know how many people are on welfare and how that relates to the total population we need to look at welfare recipients in relation to all poor people.

First we must decide how to decide who is poor. There are two basic government "systems" for looking at poverty.

The first is the **poverty line.** This is a measure of poverty developed by the Social Security Administration in 1965 (in terms of 1963 income levels) and updated each year only for rises in prices. Its most recent updating in December 1971 set the line at $4,137 for a nonfarm family of four. This measure of poverty was developed by multiplying a minimal subsistence food budget by three.

This definition of poverty is not only used in classifying persons as poor or nonpoor for statistical purposes. It also is used by the Department of Labor, Office of Economic Opportunity, and other government agencies in determining eligibility for participation in such federally aided programs as Neighborhood Youth Corps, school lunch program, etc.*

A second governmental poverty measure based on much more detailed and actual research was established by the Bureau of Labor Statistics (of the Department of Labor) in 1967. It looks at actual living costs for an **urban family** of four living under specified conditions and computes three "levels" or standards of living: "lower," "intermediate," and "higher." In the most recent revision of this study (based on autumn 1971 prices) the national averages for the three levels (**after taxes**) were:

$ 6,585	Lower
$ 9,605	Intermediate
$12,249	Higher†

---

* For further explanation of the "poverty line," see pp. 93–95.
† For geographical variation of the BLS Lower Budget before and after taxes, see p. 96.

A third measure of poverty is provided by a now annual Gallup Poll which asks: What is the smallest amount of money a family of four (husband, wife, and two children) needs each week to get along in this community? As of June 1971 the answer the public gave to that question was $126 a week ($546 a month, $6,552 a year).

HOW DOES *YOUR* INCOME COMPARE WITH

An AFDC family of four with no other income gets	$ 2,364
An AFDC family of four with average additional income gets	$ 2,784
A full-time worker at the minimum wage of $1.60 per hour gets	$ 3,320
THE POVERTY LINE	$ 4,137
The Bureau of Labor Statistics Lower Budget for a family of four is	$ 7,214
The U. S. median family income was	$10,290
The Bureau of Labor Statistics Intermediate Budget for a family of four is	$10,971
The Bureau of Labor Statistics Higher Budget for a family of four is	$15,905
Your annual family income for a family of ——— is	

Note: All of these are the most recently available figures (late 1971/early 1972).

Poverty, as measured by the lowest of these three measures, the poverty line concept ($4,137 for a family of four), had been declining during the 1960s. However, in 1970 the number of poor persons increased by about 1.2 million or 5.1 percent. **In 1970 about 25.5 million or 13 percent of the population were below the poverty level of $3,968 for a family of four.**
This means that the fifteen million people receiving welfare represent just 55 percent of those who are poor. Or to

put it the other way, only about one of every two poor people receives welfare.

The "poverty gap"—the amount of money it would take to raise the income of all poor families above the poverty line—was $11.4 billion in 1970. The average amount needed per family to "get out of poverty" was $1,100. (Source: Bureau of the Census, P-60, No. 77, May 7, 1971.)

Up to this time detailed data on poor people on a state-by-state basis has not been available. The Bureau of the Census now has and will soon publish this information based on the 1970 Census.

HOW DOES WHAT WE SPEND ON WELFARE COMPARE WITH . . . ?

We also need facts about how welfare expenditures relate to other spending and to our national, state, and local revenues.

As of January 1972 welfare expenditures totaled $1.5 billion a month or approximately $18 billion per year. This includes federal, state, and local spending for all public assistance categories and medical care for welfare recipients and other poor people. AFDC accounts for slightly more than a third of this. (Source: NCSS A-2, Jan. 1972.) (Chart below shows welfare costs for fiscal year 1970.)

HOW MUCH MONEY DOES WELFARE COST?

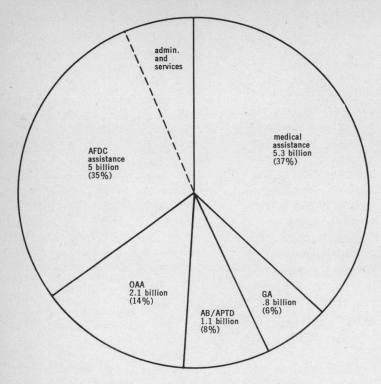

FISCAL YEAR ENDING JUNE 30, 1970

Source: NCSS F-2, 1970.

Welfare and the Federal Budget
The approximately $6 billion **federal** expenditure for welfare in 1969 represented about 3 percent of total federal spending and compared with $75 billion for military spending which was about 40 percent of the total (including $26 billion for the Vietnam war).

THE FACTS ABOUT WELFARE

According to the 1970 Federal Statistical Abstract we spent less on welfare than on alcoholic beverages ($15.6 billion) or tobacco ($9.7 billion)!

Welfare and State and Local Budgets
Available data for the fiscal year 1966–67 shows that the federal government spent approximately 4% of its general revenue for welfare. This compared with the 3% of **local** general revenue spent on welfare by local government and almost 8% of state general revenue spent on welfare by state government.

The state and local welfare fiscal burden measured in this way has remained very stable since 1960.

The question of welfare cost-sharing and the amount of burden that each level of government can or should carry is one of the most complex and critical of welfare issues. **Note:** An excellent study of these complexities is available as one of the technical studies done for the President's Commission on Income Maintenance Programs. (Source: The President's Commission on Income Maintenance Programs Technical Studies, 1970, "Income Maintenance Programs and State-Local Finances," Robert W. Rafuse, Jr., p. 219.)

WHO GETS THE FEDERAL BILLIONS*

MILITARY SPENDING:	
	$77 BILLION
Vietnam war	$26 billion
Military pensions	$ 2 billion
All other military costs	$49 billion

HEALTH AND WELFARE	
SPENDING:	$50 BILLION
Social Security pensions	$27 billion
Medicare for the aged	$ 6 billion
Welfare grants and medicaid to needy	*$ 6 billion*
Unemployment pay	$ 3 billion

OTHER CIVILIAN SPENDING:	
	$45 BILLION
Care of veterans	$ 7 billion
Highways, airports, business developments	$ 8 billion
Help for schools, colleges, students	$ 5 billion
Aid to farmers	$ 6 billion
Space exploration	$ 5 billion
Foreign affairs and economic aid	$ 5 billion
Rebuilding of cities and towns	$ 1 billion

* The figures are unofficial estimates of Fiscal Year 1969 outlays.

Antipoverty "war"..... $ 2 billion
Public-health services. $ 2 billion
Federal workers'
  pensions............ $ 2 billion
Other health and
  welfare programs... $ 2 billion

Developing atomic
  energy, including
  military and space
  projects............ $ 3 billion
Power and water
  projects, general
  government, all
  other federal costs.. $ 5 billion

INTEREST ON THE NATIONAL
   DEBT: $14 BILLION

ALL GOVERNMENT PROGRAMS:
                    $186 BILLION

Source: Reprinted from **U.S. News & World Report,** Feb. 5, 1968. Copyright 1968 U.S. News & World Report, Inc.

WHAT ARE THE FACTS ABOUT WORK? ABOUT ILLEGITIMACY?

Before looking at the myths surrounding work and illegitimacy as they relate to welfare, let us consider a few basic facts:

Work

In 1966, 73 percent of the heads of all poor families worked. Sixty percent of them worked full time. Yet they did not earn enough to get out of poverty. This is not hard to understand when you remember that full time work, forty hours a week, at the $1.60 minimum wage comes to only $3,320 a year!

Thus for many people on welfare even full-time work would not be enough to really make them "self-supporting."

One study found that about 45 percent of all AFDC mothers have "high employment potential" because of education or previous job experience. Four out of five of these mothers wanted a steady job but 80 percent could not work because they had children under eight and did not have access to day care.

THE FACTS ABOUT WELFARE

Thirty-eight percent of the mothers in this high-potential group cited poor general health as an important factor in their joblessness. (Source: Perry Levinson, "How Employable Are AFDC Women?" **Welfare in Review,** Vol. 8, No. 4, July–Aug. 1970.)

In 1969 data on highest grade of school completed for AFDC mothers showed that for the approximately 80% of AFDC mothers for whom this information was available, 22% had eighth-grade education or less, 38% had some high school, 25% had completed high school, and 4% had attended college. (Source: NCSS Report AFDC-1, 1971.)

Illegitimacy
A recent study found no link "between levels or changes in rates of illegitimacy and the number of families on AFDC or changes in benefit levels." (Source: Phillips Cutwright, "Illegitimacy: Myths, Causes and Cures," **Family Planning Perspectives,** Vol. 3, No. 1, Jan. 1971, p. 29.)

WHY ARE THE WELFARE ROLLS RISING?
Finally before we leave "the facts" let us look briefly at the growth of AFDC.

"The cost of AFDC tripled between 1960 and 1970. The number of recipients has more than doubled. In the 15 years since 1955 the proportion of children in the nation receiving assistance has doubled." (Source: Testimony of then Health, Education, and Welfare Secretary Robert H. Finch, Family Assistance Act of 1970 Hearings before the Senate Finance Committee as cited pp. 162–63.)

Why is the AFDC program growing? A recent study by HEW supplied information on factors identified by the states as contributing to increase in numbers of recipients during the twelve months ended in June 1970. These included higher assistance standards (making more people eligible), court decisions (especially regarding the "man in the house" and residence), changes in economic conditions, and greater public knowledge and awareness about the availability of assistance. (Source: NCSS Report H-4.)

There are probably many reasons why AFDC has continued to grow since 1960 in recession and upswing alike. As with many facets of the welfare program, the facts are not enough to answer **why.** They are instead, as usual, just a useful jumping-off point!

☛ DO-ITS

1. Using the form on p. 110 (or inventing your own) make a simple FACTS ON WELFARE leaflet for your state.
2. Get the basic statistics of welfare by writing to the U. S. Department of Health, Education, and Welfare, Social and Rehabilitation Service, National Center for Social Statistics for these key reports:
   NCSS A-2 Public Assistance Statistics published monthly
   NCSS A-4 Trend Report: Graphic Presentation of Public Assistance and Related Data published yearly
   NCSS A-6 Program Facts on Federally Aided Public Assistance Income Maintenance Programs published yearly
   NCSS D-2 OAA and AFDC Standards for Basic Needs published yearly
   NCSS F-2 Source of Funds Expended for Public Assistance Payments and for the Cost of Administration, Services, and Training published yearly
   NCSS H-4 Trends in AFDC 1965–1970 (on why rolls rose!)
   NCSS AFDC-2 The AFDC Family in the 1960's (compares 1961, 1967, 1969 AFDC studies)
   NCSS AFDC-1 and AFDC-2 Findings of the 1971 (most recent) AFDC study
   AFDC-1-Demographic and Program Characteristics; AFDC-2-Financial Circumstances
   NCSS H-4 (June 1971) AFDC: Selected statistical data on Families Aided and Program Operations—a compilation of the most frequently requested facts about AFDC
   NCSS reprint OAA Recipients in 1965 (summarizes most recent OAA study)
3. Also useful:
   a. from the Bureau of Labor Statistics

Three Standards of Living, **Spring 1967—Bulletin 1570-5 and USDL 72-240 Autumn 1971 revision of this dated Apr. 27, 1972.**

b. **from the Bureau of the Census**
   Series P-60, No. 82, July 18, 1972. 1971 poverty information. Also series PC (1)-C which is just being issued and will contain poverty data from 1970 census by states.

c. **from Government Printing Office (or your Congressman or Senator)** President's Commission on Income Maintenance, Poverty Amid Plenty, The American Paradox; and Background Papers and Technical Studies, 3 volumes.
   Subsidy and Subsidy Effect Programs of the U. S. Government.
   Materials Prepared for the Joint Economic Committee, 89th Congress, First Session 41-788, Joint Committee Print

Note: **There are usually three ways to obtain government publications:**

1. **FREE—write to your Congressman or Senator. This also communicates your interest in the subject.**
2. **FREE—write to the government agency. It will usually be able to send you single copies only.**
3. **For those committed to self-support, PAY by** ordering from the Government Printing Office, Washington, D.C. 20402.

What Are the Facts About Old People on Welfare?

As of January 1972 two million old persons were receiving old-age assistance. This comprised 13% of all welfare recipients. In terms of cost OAA (old age assistance) represented 18% of the total money payments for public assistance in January 1972. Just over 100 of each 1,000 persons over sixty-five years old receive OAA. The average monthly OAA payment is $77.37. States with average grants over $100 per month are Alaska, California, Hawaii, Iowa, Massachusetts, New Hampshire, New York, and Wisconsin. States with average payments less than $60 per month are Florida, Georgia, Indiana, Kansas, Kentucky, Mississippi, Nebraska, New Mexico, Rhode Island, South Carolina, Tennessee, Texas, and Wyoming.

Only a third (versus 54% for AFDC) of OAA recipients live in the most populated states and 40% (versus 20% for AFDC) live in the South. Only 46% live in urban areas (versus 70% for AFDC).

In 1965 (most recent study) :
- over 75% of OAA recipients were white (versus 51% AFDC)
- only 22% were black (versus 45% AFDC)
- two-thirds were women
- 1 in 4 was married and living with a husband or wife
- nearly half owned (or were buying) their own home (versus 17% AFDC)
- 1 in 8 had a child contributing support
- only 1 in 6 was confined to the home because of physical or mental conditions
- average time on OAA was 6 years
- almost half also received Social Security (OASDI) payments
- nearly 40% lived alone

For the fiscal year ending June 30, 1970, OAA recipients received a total of about $1.9 billion.

Of this 65% came from federal funds, 31% from state funds and 4% from local funds (versus 54%, 35%, 11% for AFDC).

It cost $212 million for administration services and training for the OAA program, or approximately 10% (versus 17% AFDC).

Source :   NCSS Report,
           Old Age Recipients in 1965 and 1969,
           and OAA data in NCSS Reports,
           cited for AFDC facts.

HOW MANY PEOPLE IN YOUR STATE RECEIVE OLD AGE ASSISTANCE?

State	Number of Recipients	State	Number of Recipients
Total.........	2,018,667	Mont.............	3,241
		Nebr. (1)........	7,280
Ala...............	113,197	Nev.............	2,891
Alaska (1).......	1,947		
Ariz..............	13,366	N.H.............	4,571
Ark. (1)..........	58,236	N.J. (2)..........	19,500
Calif.............	314,064	N. Mex. (1)......	8,560
Colo..............	31,111	N.Y. (1).........	110,513
Conn.............	8,115	N.C. (1).........	35,213
Del...............	2,788	N. Dak. (1)......	3,707
D.C...............	4,202	Ohio.............	51,286
Fla. (1)..........	56,139	Okla. (1).........	67,692
		Oreg.............	7,548
Ga. (1)..........	90,720	Pa...............	50,389
Guam............	460		
Hawaii (1).......	2,699	P.R. (1).........	20,536
Idaho............	3,327	R.I. (1)..........	3,911
Ill. (1)...........	33,822	S.C..............	17,489
Ind..............	16,045	S. Dak...........	3,683
Iowa.............	21,984	Tenn.............	49,699
Kans. (1)........	9,926	Tex..............	210,462
Ky. (1)...........	58,037	Utah.............	2,859
La................	115,311	Vt. (1)...........	4,162
		V.I...............	325
Maine (1).......	10,774	Va...............	14,171
Md. (1)..........	9,456		
Mass.............	57,316	Wash............	19,172
Mich.............	41,408	W. Va............	11,899
Minn.............	17,192	Wis..............	19,602
Miss.............	81,241	Wyo.............	1,412
Mo...............	94,011		

(1) Represents aid to the aged under program for Aid to the Aged, Blind, and Disabled.
(2) Estimated by state.

Source: NCSS Report,
Jan. 1972.

HOW MUCH DO OAA RECIPIENTS NEED AND HOW MUCH DO THEY GET?

Old Age Assistance: *Full Monthly Standard for Basic Needs for an Aged Woman* (1), *Largest Amount That Can Be Paid to Such Recipients* (1), by State, and Average Grant (2)

	Full Standard	Largest Amount Paid	Average
Ala..................	$146	$103	$ 67.41
Alaska............	250	250	128.68
Ariz...............	118	118	72.50
Ark................	109	105	65.78
Calif..............	178	178	110.42
Colo..............	140	140	74.86
Conn..............	169	169	98.50
Del................	140	140	94.62
D.C...............	204	153	94.35
Fla.................	114	114	58.70
Ga.................	105	91	55.52
Guam.............	(3)	(3)	69.38
Hawaii............	132	132	100.74
Idaho.............	163	163	75.22
Ill.................	169	169	67.41
Ind................	185	100	57.74
Iowa..............	122	117	127.69
Kan...............	208	203	49.60
Ky.................	96	96	59.39
La.................	143	100	73.79
Maine.............	123	115	63.90
Md................	130	96	66.16
Mass.............	189	189	104.21
Mich..............	224	224	79.65
Minn..............	183	183	75.43
Miss..............	150	75	58.42
Mo................	181	85	75.90
Mont..............	120	111	63.90
Neb...............	182	182	58.78
Nev...............	170	170	72.94
N.H...............	173	173	166.73
N.J...............	(4) 142	(4) 142	89.49
N. Mex...........	116	116	54.39
N.Y...............	159	159	106.62
N.C...............	112	112	72.96
N.D...............	(4) 125	(4) 125	91.44
Ohio..............	126	126	61.96

(1) July 1971.
(2) Jan. 1972.
(3) Data not reported.
(4) Flat allowance; includes special needs.

THE FACTS ABOUT WELFARE

	Full Standard	Largest Amount Paid	Average
Okla...............	130	130	68.73
Ore...............	153	122	60.97
Pa.................	146	146	98.03
P.R...............	54	22	18.24
R.I................	163	163	59.30
S.C...............	87	80	49.03
S.D...............	180	180	62.35
Tenn..............	102	97	49.84
Texas.............	119	119	54.34
Utah..............	151	103	62.54
Vt.................	177	177	75.31
V.I................	52	52	46.31
Va................	152	152	69.66
Wash.............	143	143	62.25
W. Va.............	146	76	98.05
Wis...............	158	158	134.96
Wyo...............	139	104	56.23

Sources: Monthly standard and largest amount paid:
NCSS Report D-2 (SRS 72-03200), July 1971.
Average grants data:
NCSS Report A-2, Jan. 1972.

EXPENDITURES FOR OAA AND PERCENTAGE OF FUNDS FROM FEDERAL GOVERNMENT, STATE, LOCAL GOVERNMENT—FISCAL YEAR ENDING JUNE 30, 1970

State	Amount in Millions	% Federal Funds	% State Funds	% Local Funds
Alabama..............	104	75.7	24.2	.1
Alaska...............	3	47.9	52.1	...
Arizona..............	13	74.5	25.2	.2
Arkansas............	50	78.4	21.6	...
California............	457	51.1	39.2	9.6
Colorado............	37	65.3	31.9	2.7
Connecticut.........	10	49.0	51.0	...
Delaware............	2	65.4	34.6	...
Dist. of Columbia....	4	57.0	43.0	...
Florida..............	61	72.4	27.6	...
Georgia..............	63	83.3	13.4	3.3
Guam................		50.8	49.2	...
Hawaii..............	3	49.5	50.5	...
Idaho...............	3	67.8	32.1	.1
Illinois..............	40	65.1	34.9	...

State	Amount in Millions	% Federal Funds	% State Funds	% Local Funds
Indiana...............	23	53.2	28.2	18.7
Iowa.................	36	55.9	43.8	.3
Kansas..............	16	58.0	22.3	19.6
Kentucky............	46	79.5	20.5	...
Louisiana............	103	73.9	26.1	...
Maine...............	9	73.6	26.4	...
Maryland............	7	76.4	16.2	7.4
Massachusetts......	63	49.7	50.3	(1)
Michigan............	37	50.0	49.9	.1
Minnesota...........	21	57.6	23.2	19.2
Mississippi..........	46	79.6	20.2	.3
Missouri.............	94	67.4	32.6	(1)
Montana............	4	66.2	21.5	12.3
Nebraska............	7	73.6	26.4	...
Nevada..............	3	65.2	34.8	...
New Hampshire.....	7	58.7	17.2	24.0
New Jersey..........	19	57.0	29.0	13.9
New Mexico.........	7	82.0	18.0	...
New York............	142	52.4	24.2	23.4
North Carolina.......	36	74.3	13.4	12.3
North Dakota........	5	68.6	24.5	7.0
Ohio.................	49	67.1	30.3	2.6
Oklahoma...........	67	77.6	22.4	...
Oregon..............	6	55.6	44.4	...
Pennsylvania........	59	54.5	45.5	...
Puerto Rico..........		48.1	51.9	...
Rhode Island........	3	64.4	35.6	...
South Carolina......	13	75.7	23.7	.6
South Dakota........	4	66.5	33.0	.5
Tennessee..........	40	75.9	19.8	4.4
Texas................	182	74.2	25.7	.1
Utah.................	3	68.5	31.4	.1
Vermont.............	4	64.9	35.1	...
Virgin Islands........		49.2	50.8	...
Virginia..............	11	64.4	19.0	16.6
Washington.........	20	50.3	49.7	...
West Virginia........	12	73.5	26.5	...
Wisconsin...........	24	54.6	26.4	18.9
Wyoming............	2	70.1	12.8	17.2

(1) Less than 0.05%.

Source: NCSS Report F-2,
Fiscal Year 1970.

THE FACTS ABOUT WELFARE

THE POVERTY LINE

WHAT IS IT?

According to 1970 guidelines set by the OEO, the poverty line for a nonfarm family of four is $3,800 in yearly income, or about $73 a week.

The new guidelines are $100 to $200 a year above 1969 limits for families of various sizes, but this is strictly a reflection of the steep increases in our basic living costs. The raises do not in any way consider higher living standards.

Family Size	A Week	A Month	A Year
1	$35.54	$153	$1,900
2	48.08	197	2,500
3	59.62	256	3,100
4	73.08	317	3,800
5	84.62	364	4,400
6	96.15	412	5,000
7	107.69	463	5,600

Source: OEO Income
Poverty Guidelines 12–1–70.

Note: 1971 OEO guideline is $4,000 for a family of four.

WHAT DOES IT PROVIDE?

Possible monthly budget for family of four	Amount
food	$136
housing	101
transportation	7
clothing and personal care	63
medical care	
other consumption (recreation, education, tobacco, etc.)	10
Total	$317

HOW IS IT FIGURED?

Unfortunately, the department's food plan, the basis of the poverty index, is not very realistic. It is estimated that only about a fourth of the families who spend that much for food actually have a nutritionally adequate diet.

The poverty index is simply this food budget multiplied by three to reflect the fact that food typically represents a third of the expenses of a low-income family.

FOOD

This food budget requires more than a third of the poor family's income, but still allows only a dollar a day for food per person.

SHELTER

The poor family's budget provides only $101 a month for all housing costs—including rent, utilities, and household operation—for four persons. No allowance is included for the poor family to purchase household furnishings. In Head Start programs, for example, teachers found that many children never had eaten at a table. Thirty percent of families on welfare live in homes where each family member does not have a bed.

CLOTHING

Clothing school children is a major problem in poor families. Many poor children wear hand-me-down clothes which they receive from relatives, neighbors, and even teachers. Some clothing may be purchased at secondhand stores. But many poor children have to go to school on rainy days with no boots or raincoats, or stay home.

TRANSPORTATION

The money allotted to transportation for a poor family would not cover even daily transportation for a worker. The moderate-income family not only has more money to spend on recreation, but its automobile permits it to take the children on inexpensive outings, while poor children rarely have access to any form of transportation. Thus, many poor children have never left their own neighborhoods.

LUXURIES

The poor family has $120 annually—about $10 a month—to spend on "luxuries"—reading material, education, gifts and contributions, tobacco, alcohol. But it is likely that this money will be spent on necessities, supplementing the meager food, clothing, and housing allowances. There is no room in the budget for luxuries or emergencies.

ANYTHING ELSE

Technically, an income at the poverty level should enable families to purchase the bare necessities of life. Yet an itemized budget drawn at that level clearly falls short of adequacy. There are many items for which no money is budgeted, although those items may be needed. *Funds for them can only come out of sums already allotted to the basic necessities of life.*

HOW DOES IT WORK?

As one witness told the commission, "I either eat good and smell bad, or smell good and don't eat." When another witness was asked how he made ends meet, he simply replied, "They don't meet."

> Source: *Poverty Amid Plenty: An American Paradox,* The Report of President's Commission on Income Maintenance, 1969, pp. 14–16.

BUREAU OF LABOR STATISTICS LOWER LIVING STANDARD FOR A FAMILY OF FOUR, AUTUMN 1971 NONFARM

Area	Total Budget (includes income taxes and social security)	Comparative Index
Urban United States.................	$ 7,214	$100
Metropolitan areas....................	7,330	102
Nonmetropolitan areas...............	6,694	93
Northeast:		
Boston, Mass...........................	7,825	108
Buffalo, N.Y...........................	7,277	101
Hartford, Conn........................	7,920	110
New York-Northeastern New Jersey..	7,578	105
Philadelphia, Pa.-N.J.................	7,406	103
Nonmetropolitan areas...............	7,052	98
North Central:		
Cedar Rapids, Iowa...................	7,033	97
Chicago, Ill.-Northwestern Ind........	7,536	104
Cincinnati, Ohio-Ky.-Ind...............	6,854	95
Cleveland, Ohio.......................	7,230	100
Detroit, Mich..........................	7,074	98
Indianapolis, Ind......................	7,231	100
Kansas City, Mo.-Kansas.............	7,241	100
Milwaukee, Wis.......................	7,285	101
Minneapolis-St. Paul, Minn...........	7,233	100
St. Louis, Mo.-Ill.....................	7,238	100
Nonmetropolitan areas...............	6,943	96
South:		
Atlanta, Ga............................	6,681	93
Baton Rouge, La......................	6,362	91
Durham, N.C..........................	7,009	97
Houston, Tex..........................	6,686	93
Nashville, Tenn.......................	6,584	91
Orlando, Fla...........................	6,786	94
Washington, D.C.-Md.-Va.............	7,500	104
Nonmetropolitan areas...............	6,267	87
West:		
Denver, Colo..........................	6,818	95
Los Angeles-Long Beach, Calif........	7,671	106
San Francisco-Oakland, Calif..........	7,971	111
Seattle-Everett, Wash.................	7,666	106
Honolulu, Hawaii......................	8,990	125
Nonmetropolitan areas...............	7,199	100
Anchorage, Alaska....................	11,019	153

Source: Bureau of Labor Statistics,
USDL 72-240,
Apr. 27, 1972.

HOW THE BUREAU OF LABOR STATISTICS
LOWER LEVEL OF LIVING BUDGET IS FIGURED

1. The family consists of an employed husband, age thirty-eight, a wife not employed outside the home, an eight-year-old girl, and a thirteen-year-old boy.

2. Housing costs include utilities—the family is assumed to rent.

3. Transportation costs are based on averaging automobile owners' and nonowners' costs.

4. The 1971 budgets were derived by applying price changes as reported in the consumer price index to the previous data. Full information on methods of calculation, quantities of goods and services, etc. can be obtained from *Three Standards of Living for an Urban Family of Four Persons,* BLS Bulletin 1570-5, Spring 1967, $1 GPO.

5. The autumn 1971 average lower budget for a family of four— $7,214—was derived as follows:

food	$1,964
housing	1,516
transportation	536
clothing and personal care	848
medical care	609
other family consumption	368
other items (gifts, contributions, life insurance, and occupational expenses)	357
social security	387
personal income taxes	629
Total	$7,214

WHAT IS IT LIKE TO LIVE
ON A WELFARE BUDGET?

When asked what they did about running out of money two-thirds said they borrowed, either from relatives and friends or store-keepers, and one-third said they just "stayed run out." "Stay run out" is the theme of their lives—and for those who borrow too, because the loan must be paid back, and each month they sink a little deeper. Besides borrowing and staying run out, some found other ways to cope with the continuing crisis: One "lets the bills go." (Where does this end?) One cashes in bottles and borrows food. One cried in shame: "The lady downstairs gives us food." One said, "If the children get sick, I call the police to take them to Receiving Hospital."

One has been "borrowing" secretly from the funds of a Ladies' Club of which she is treasurer. The club is her one meaningful adult social contact. There is soon to be an election for new club officers and she will be exposed. Her children ask, "Mama, why are you always so sad?" Half crazy with worry, she feels sick; at Receiving Hospital they have referred her to the psychiatrist.

One was in despair because a retarded son who delights in his monthly visit home from the County Training School was coming tomorrow, and there was little food and no money or food stamps in the house. One said bitterly, "A woman could always get $10 if she had to. I prefer not to resort to this."

Consider our affluent society: in an economy generating wealth sufficient to supply every family of four with nearly $10,000 per year income, we reduce a family to cashing in pop bottles to get food, we push a woman to thoughts of prostitution to feed her children, we force an honest woman into theft and then provide her with $25-an-hour psychiatric treatment.

What do these reasonable rent and utility costs mean to an AFDC family? Consider a mother with two children. Say that rent and utilities are $70 per month. Out of their $140 grant that leaves $70. But the state welfare department says that three people need $102 a month for food and incidentals. It is clear that for these families "something suffers."

One mother, three days after receipt of her check (and twelve days before the next one would come), had 56¢ left. She had bought food and coal and paid the rent, but held off on the gas and electricity bills because there was no money to pay them. The gas and electricity may be cut off, she says, as they have been twice in the last two years. And what of school supplies, clothing, or carfare?

About eight out of ten boys have but one pair of shoes; about half the girls have only one pair of shoes, and half have two pairs. About half the children have no rubbers or boots of any kind, and about three-fourths have no raincoats of any description.

Source: Charles Lebeaux, "Life on ADC: Budgets of Despair," *New University Thought,* Vol. 3, No. 4, 1963. Used by permission.

"THE MAIN PROBLEM IS MONEY"

The main problem is money . . . that is our main problem, money. . . . But even with my working, the money I get from work and the money I get on AFDC, it is still not sufficient to live decently.

Source: "A Time To Listen . . . A Time To Act," a report of U. S. Commission on Civil Rights, Nov. 1967.

Here is someone like you who tried to find out what it's like to live on welfare.

WEAK ON WELFARE
By June Rossbach Bingham '41*

In 30 years, my husband and I never had a serious argument about money. Then we, together with several other Congressional families, were "invited" by the National Welfare Rights Organization to live for a week on the equivalent of the welfare allotment in our home state.

* Reprinted from **Barnard Alumnae,** Winter 1970. Used by permission.

I was sitting at the kitchen table with cookbooks and newspaper advertisements, trying to figure to the penny the cost of 21 low-income meals, when my husband called from the next room, "Be sure to leave enough for a beer."

"Beer?" I shouted. "You can't have a beer."

His face in the doorway would have chilled the beer. "I'd like to know why I can't have one can of beer."

"We can't afford it."

"Don't be silly."

"I'm not silly: 28 cents is silly. I can't make 28 cents cover our food, let alone soap, toilet tissue, deodorant . . ."

"Where did you get that figure of 28 cents?"

"It's New York's allotment per person per meal."

"Oh no it isn't."

"What are you talking about?"

"It's been cut."

"*Cut?* It can't be cut. It has to be bigger. 28 doesn't give us meat or fish even every second day."

He sighed. "Sorry, but you'll have to figure on 22."

"I can't!"

"Listen. People in Washington, D.C. have only 17 cents. People in Arkansas have only 8 cents; people in Mississippi have only 4 cents."

I put my hands over my ears.

He turned and left the room.

"And prices are going *up,*" I wailed.

"Hurry, then," he called back. "You might still fit in one can of . . ."

"No beer," I shouted. And there was a new taste of venom on my tongue.

As the day approached for Welfare Budget Week to start, we confessed to each other that we were dreading it more than we had thought. Mutual reassurance helped but little; it was true that we had previously lived for weeks in the Far East on little more than rice and condiments, bread and tea. But that was different; there, we had been in tune with the majority; here, we would be out of tune with it. Also, we began to understand the ferocity with which people in the low-income areas have often resisted any enforced scientific improvement in their food habits. Like a person's handwriting, his characteristic diet feels to him like a hallmark of the self, a component of his identity. When it is threatened from the outside, a surprisingly basic form of anxiety seems to be mobilized.

At the briefing for the participants in Welfare Budget Week, a staff representative of NWRO had mentioned the wide variety of excuses offered by invitees who not only did not wish to take part in the experiment but also, apparently, did not wish to say so directly. Perhaps one reason for their reluctance, so variously rationalized, was precisely the discomfort of this anxiety. I found myself haunted by the statement of a student leader on the *Generations Apart* television program: "Comfortability is a very dangerous god." On the other hand, in many countries of Europe, I consoled myself by thinking, a comparable group of people would have responded to such an invitation with disbelief or disdain.

Like prisoners on Death Row my husband and I had a ceremonial "last meal." It cost almost as much as the $9.24 (66 cents per person per day) that would cover all food and sundries for the following week. Unlike the prisoners, we enjoyed every bite of the steak and broccoli hollandaise, the fresh peaches with cream, the bottle of wine. Not only did we disregard cost and calorie count, but also cholesterol. For, as I had discovered through my menu-making, one backhanded advantage of a low-cost diet is that the high cholesterol foods, such as eggs and butter, "marbled" beef and shell-fish, are out of the question, while low cholesterol foods, such as the legumes (including vegetarian baked beans) and canned fish must, for the reason of price, be the chief source of protein.

Our first breakfast was typical (except for Sunday when we had pancakes and syrup): a small glass of grapefruit juice (large can 41 cents), oatmeal with reconstituted milk, and coffee with the same milk (15 cents a quart and good).

Since my husband could no longer afford lunch at one of the

MENUS

7 Breakfasts

6 days — grapefruit juice, oatmeal, powdered milk, coffee

Sunday — tomato juice, pancakes with syrup, coffee

7 Lunches

Thurs. (7/17) — peanut butter with jelly sandwich (1 each)
— 1 tuna salad sandwich
— 1 banana for husband

Fri. (7/18) — 1 egg salad sandwich (husband)
— 1 french toast (myself)
— 1 raw carrot (husband)
— 1 parboiled celery (myself)

Sat. (7/19) — chicken wings with rice braised lettuce

Sun. (7/20) — meat loaf with oatmeal raw carrots

Mon. (7/21) — 2 meat loaf sandwiches (1 for each of us) raw carrots biscuits with jelly banana for husband

Tues. (7/22) — 2 tuna salad sandwiches (1 for each)

Wed. (7/23) — 2 tomato and cheese and meatloaf sandwiches (1 for each)

7 Suppers

Thurs. (7/17) — baked California lima beans—with tomato juice and onion, celery and carrot braised lettuce
— snack before bed—Jello and biscuits

Fri. (7/18) — veal kidney with soup scraps spaghetti cooked lettuce

Sat. (7/19) — baked beans raw carrot (lunch was larger than usual) banana and orange

Sun. (7/20) — soup with rest of rice and lettuce (lunch large) biscuit
— moon feast—cheese and biscuits; cold meat loaf; Kool Aid

Mon. (7/21) — mackerel cakes cabbage cooked in chicken bouillon biscuit

Tues. (7/22) — rest of kidney rice and rest of beans gelatin vegetable salad

Wed. (7/23) — pepper stuffed with rest of meat loaf plus gravy from soup fat

Capitol restaurants, I gave him sandwiches, together with a raw carrot, and a bruised banana (4 cents, reduced). In return, he promised to bring home all baggies and pieces of Saran wrap to be washed and re-used, although I resented devoting any of our precious detergent for this purpose; finally I learned to leave a pot of soapy water in the sink all day.

The welfare mothers at the NWRO briefing had offered various suggestions. One was to buy day-old bread at half price. But the markets within walking distance of our house do not carry it. Instead, a bakery truck comes daily and picks it up to be resold at a discount store miles away. The saving on bread, for a family of two, would not have been sufficient to pay my carfare. Bread, therefore, was too expensive (1½ cents per slice) to use for *my*

THE FACTS ABOUT WELFARE

lunch. In its place I baked biscuits (using the self-rising flour recommended by the welfare mothers) and tried to make the sandwich filling stay between their halves. For the first two days this filling was peanut butter and jelly, a high carbohydrate taste-thrill that we do not ordinarily permit ourselves. But it "held" us less well than did the subsequent tunafish salad. After the weekend, we had for sandwiches slices of meatloaf (stretched with oatmeal) which tasted so grim when cold that I blew 40 cents from my dollar emergency fund for half a pound of American cheese and 8 cents for a bruised tomato with which to dress these up. The tastelessness and monotony of the foods available on welfare became depressing even though we were on it merely for one week.

A further item of advice given by a welfare mother, to buy luncheon meats and hot dogs, I decided to disregard because of their relative expense and dearth of protein. Our meatloaf came cheap because we waited until late Saturday afternoon, shortly before the market closed for the weekend, to buy hamburger at half price (50 cents). We also received free from the butcher a soup bone he would otherwise have thrown away. Previously I had procured from the man who prepares fresh vegetables for display the lettuce, cabbage, and celery "trimmings" that would otherwise have rotted in the garbage can. With two beef bouillon cubes (two cents apiece) I boiled the washed, ungritted outer lettuce leaves. They were delicious. The celery and cabbage, on the other hand, were almost too tough to eat, even after having been boiled. I was able, however, to salvage enough celery for the tuna salad sandwich filling and enough cabbage to serve once as hot vegetable. Potatoes were tempting to buy, but too expensive, as compared with the spaghetti and rice on which we filled ourselves—for a couple of hours at least.

The main trouble with a diet made up mostly of starch is that one is subject to flash-hungers between meals. Without warning, one is not merely hungry; one is ravenous, hurting, unable to concentrate on anything except getting something into the stomach. We both drank more water than usual, sometimes mixed with Kool Aid (five cents for several quarts). We also kept an emergency supply of biscuits in pocket or pocketbook or even, on Sunday, in our golf bags.

This type of hunger appears, moreover, to be cumulative. The first day we felt it not at all. Indeed, there was a slight euphoria that stemmed perhaps from at last being engaged in meeting the challenge, rather than merely dreading it. We got through the morning nicely on our oatmeal, and enjoyed our peanut butter and jelly for lunch. That night we had California limas (baked with Worcestershire sauce, tomato juice, and onion—a total of 18 cents) and some of our "braised" lettuce. But at bedtime we discovered we were too hungry to sleep. Having long outgrown the habit of a midnight snack, we found ourselves deep into dishes of Jello (2½ cents apiece), and biscuits. Psychologically, those biscuits were as important as physically because, like the lettuce, they were something of which we could have all we wanted.

By the third day, however, we were not getting through the morning without hunger pangs. Yet we could not afford whole milk or cream or eggs for breakfast. The ration of six small eggs for the week was needed for cooking. A 29-cent can of mackerel, for example, can be mixed with egg and flour, the egg serving to bind the fish together; this can then be made into patties and sauteed as a good main dish for supper. Belatedly, we realized that our comparative comfort that first day could be credited less to the welfare breakfast than to the carry-over from our pre-welfare "last supper."

During the latter half of the week, despite added quantities of oatmeal for breakfast, I found myself frequently empty, as against consciously hungry, and too lethargic to force myself to the typewriter. Even when I gave up my quarter-century routine of morning hours at the desk and instead tried to read some of the serious books necessary to the career of a free-lance writer, my mind wandered off, not "wool"-gathering, but food-gathering. Accompanying the loss of concentration was a loss of physical energy. In place of an afternoon swim or tennis game, I stayed flat on the bed, partly because walking the requisite distance (two blocks) seemed like too much work, partly be-

THE FACTS ABOUT WELFARE

cause exercise would whet my already too great appetite, and partly because I did not feel up to the effort of casual conversation, especially since some people were so antagonistic to our Welfare Week experiment. One upper-income acquaintance termed our participation "a cheap political trick." One lower-income acquaintance told of a neighbor who cheats on welfare.

My eschewing company, nonetheless, was a mistake. While I was undergoing an unpleasant combination of loneliness and fear of people, my husband, on Capitol Hill, was constantly stimulated by his contacts with constituents, office staff, and fellow legislators, even when they disagreed with him. At the end of the day he was hungry and tired but fulfilled, while I was debilitated and frustrated. How on earth, we asked each other, can people be expected to get off welfare when they cannot afford to buy the proteins and vitamins, the so-called "brain foods," that energize? We began to understand better the report that some children on welfare fell asleep in class, or mooned out the window.

Besides thinking far more than usual about food by day, I dreamed of it by night. During the first part of the week my dreams featured roast beef (rare); by the latter part, they were down to biscuits.

I learned the hard way that the best time to prepare supper is right after breakfast; otherwise the cook is too tempted to "taste" the dish half to death. (The kinds of foods demanded by welfare also tend to take longer to cook than the more expensive kinds). Probably because I so much wanted to cheat, I became compulsive about keeping a scrupulous fairness in regard to our food supplies. Anything I nibbled during the day had its counterpart saved for my husband. And the evening he casually reported he had bought a five cent box of raisins, I carried on as if he had had a beer. (One form of cheating we did indulge in was to pretend that we had given our dog away while actually keeping her at home and dispensing her usual canned dog food; it was all I could do not to cadge a bit; all that lovely meat and fat! Later, we found out that the sale of pet food in some ghetto areas far outruns the supply of pets.)

What would I be doing, I wondered, if our four children were still small or teenage, forever rifling the refrigerator? What would I say (or scream?) if they spilled their milk or absentmindedly drank up the juice for the next day's breakfast? What would I offer (besides biscuits and Kool Aid) if they arrived from school with the usual parched and starving friends? How could I deafen them to the pied piper of the Good Humor bell without making myself into a witch straight out of Endor? I began to appreciate how much of family harmony is dependent on middle-class privileges (shared by farmers of lesser means) such as room enough for one's near and dear not to be too near when they are not very dear, and a certain spontaneity about food. Is this not one more maddening example of "to him who hath, it shall be given"?

As I bargain-hunted in the market, I found a balefulness growing within myself toward those well-dressed, well-exercised women who were idly plopping a big chunk of meat, a pile of frozen vegetables, and a veritable still-life of fresh fruits into their baskets. How dared they be so unthinking in regard to their affluence? The fact that, a week before, I had been among their number, made me more, not less, critical of their apparent smugness. I was on a "trip," not psychedelically or geographically, but socio-economically, and I began to identify with my new colleagues, not only the welfare poor and the working poor, but the youthful rebels. If the occupational hazard of lifelong poverty is a chip on the shoulder, the occupational hazard of lifelong affluence is insensitivity.

Our grown son phoned one evening. "Are you gaining in spiritual insight?" he asked.

"No," I said. "I'm deep in the sin of pride. Now that I recognize the soft underbelly of American life, I look down on the fat-cats who don't."

"I see what you mean," he said.

"And I'm furious. Here is our country, capable of growing enough food for everyone, and yet we still have hunger. Hunger must be stopped!"

The following day, the rage which I thought had reached its

peak took another surge upward. In the daily newspaper which I scrounged from a neighbor's pile of discarded printed matter (thus saving ten cents), the following item revived the nightmare horror of the Great Depression:

Farmers in Oregon, Idaho and Washington have begun plowing under part of their potato crops in an effort to reverse a decline in prices.

Glen Eppich, chairman of the Adams County, Washington, unit of the National Farmers Organization, said potato prices dropped $15 a ton after the Department of Agriculture reported that about 3 per cent of the nation's potato crop is surplus.

The department's report was followed by a National Farmer's Organization call for a 4 per cent cutback. In Oregon, an estimated 1,000 acres of potatoes were destroyed, and officials in the Columbia basin of Washington estimated that 400 to 500 acres were ploughed under at a cost to farmers of about $350,000. Idaho reported crop destruction in several counties.

Intellectually, I know that the parity problem is a complex and difficult one. But then, so was putting men on the moon. When I can't buy potatoes because they are too expensive, and farmers are paid to plow them under, so as to make them more expensive, something is wrong, not only economically but humanly. If the astronauts have taught us anything, it is that we no longer have an excuse to leave our human problems unsolved.

As my husband ascertained, there were surplus foods available to welfare families in New York. But the distribution center for our area was a considerable distance from our house, was open only a few days a month, and provided a package for two which weighed 73 pounds. I, with a fused spine, cannot carry 73 pounds on a subway or bus (or anywhere else), nor can the majority (95 per cent) of people on welfare who comprise the aged, the infirm, the mothers of small children, and the children themselves. They, moreover, unlike me, do not have ready access to a car.

In most parts of the U.S. there is either a surplus commodity distribution program or a food stamp program, but not both. New York's surplus food allotment has recently been somewhat, though inadequately, improved. Where food stamps are available the family has been compelled to turn its entire "food" allotment into them. Not a penny can be saved out for emergency supplies that are not on the stamp-redeemable list, such as aspirin.

And aspirin, I found, was being eaten by me almost like peanuts, although ordinarily my average is less than one a month. Daily, starting the fourth day of welfare, I was suffering sharp, uncharacteristic headaches. After the week—and the headaches —were safely past, I phoned the family doctor to ask what might have caused the pain. "Two things," he said. One was the culture shock of a radically changed diet, particularly since the new one was high in starches. This culture shock, presumably, would not be suffered by most people on welfare. The second item was one which they might well share, namely, the self-rising flour in the biscuits which increases the sodium in the body and thus encourages the retention of fluids. Further evidence for his hypothesis was the fact, the unkindest cut of all, that after living with hunger for a week I had *gained* a pound!

After I had lost my pound and regained my composure, I phoned to report to the welfare adviser whose acquaintance I had made at the NWRO meeting. She was particularly interested in the free soup bones and the vegetable trimmings and set about checking the supermarkets in the ghetto to find out if this mutually beneficial arrangement could be duplicated. When last heard from, the two big chain stores said they would not only give away these items but would advertise the fact. So perhaps in a small way, some of the terrible wastefulness that goes on in the United States at the human level as well as the material one, may be mitigated as a result of our short experiment.

The first morning after Welfare Week I had an egg, a whole egg, a large egg, for breakfast.

It gave me indigestion.

I think, perhaps it always will . . .

EXPENSES OF REPRESENTATIVE AND MRS. JONATHAN BINGHAM ON WELFARE DIET JULY 17 THROUGH 23, 1969

Food	Cost	Food	Cost
2 small box raisins	$ .10	bread	.25
grapefruit juice	.41	mazola—⅔ bottle (47¢)	.32
Quaker oats ⅔ of 65¢ box	.45	margarine—½ lb.	.15
coffee	.79	teabags (2)	.03
powdered milk—2 qt.	.30	½ lb. onions (10¢ a lb.)	.05
rice—½ box	.10	1½ packs Kool Aid	.15
peanut butter—⅓ jar	.15	½ pack cigarettes	.20
syrup—¼ bottle (.25)	.09	spaghetti	.10
jelly—½ jar	.16	6 eggs	.30
1 bunch of carrots	.15	self-rising flour—½ lb.	.09
bananas—4 speckled	.18	pancake flour—1 cup	.15
orange—1	.08	Ivory soap	.09
½ price Sat. hamburger—		toilet tissue	.10
1¼ lb.	.50	1 soft tomato	.10
veal kidney (1 lb.)	.41	detergent	.15
chicken wings and 2 drum-		Jello	.10
sticks	.50	dried limas	.30
beef bouillon cubes (5)	.10	1 lemon	.05
chicken bouillon cubes (5)	.10	1 salad gelatin	.10
tomato juice for cooking	.19	cheese—6 oz. American	.40
Worcestershire sauce 1¼ oz.	.20	salt—pepper—sugar	.04
tuna (1 can)	.39	baked beans—can	.18
mayonnaise	.20	canned mackerel	.29
aspirin	.10		$9.24

Obtained free: trimmings from lettuce, cabbage, celery, soup bones (marrow used for gravy), 2 broken green peppers

FACTS ABOUT WELFARE IN _____
(your state)

(You can get all the information for the blanks from the charts in this book; see pages indicated.)

As of January 1972 there were _____ people receiving AFDC. This was _____ families made up of _____ children and _____ parents. This means that our state had _____% of the total AFDC caseload (p. 70).

The average AFDC payment in our state was _____ per month per recipient compared with $51.97 nationally. Our state ranks _____ nationally in AFDC payments (pp. 76–77).

We say a family of four with no other income needs a minimum of _____ per month but our maximum AFDC payment for such a family is _____ (pp. 76–77).

The Bureau of Labor Statistics says it really takes a family of four _____ to live decently in our area (p. 96).

In fiscal 1970 our state spent _____ for AFDC. This was _____% of the national AFDC expenditure. _____% of this came from state funds and _____% from local funds (versus 55.6% federal, 32.8% state, and 11.6% local nationally). See pp. 73–74.

As of January 1972 there were _____ old people receiving OAA in our state. This was _____% of the national total on OAA (p. 89).

OAA recipients get _____ per month per person in our state compared with $77.37 nationally (pp. 90–91).

We say an old person needs _____ per month to live but we only pay _____ maximum (pp. 90–91).

In fiscal 1970 we spent _____ on OAA. This was _____% of the national OAA expenditure. _____% came from federal funds, _____% from state funds and _____% from local funds (compared with 63.9% federal, 30.7% state, and 5.4% local nationally). See pp. 91–92.

You can get all this information from the charts in this book, as indicated.

☞ CHAPTER FOUR
THE WELFARE MYTHS

Now armed with history and facts we are ready to look at the "conventional wisdom" about welfare: the welfare myths.

Myths have a purpose. Generally that purpose is to keep things the way they are. Welfare myths and stereotypes are no exception.

However, in addition to the welfare myths—about work, immorality, race, and migration, "the welfare Cadillac," and welfare fraud—there are "countermyths" or oft-repeated "answers" to welfare myths which must also be examined if we are to be able to move toward the "truth about welfare."

We have already carefully cited a great many facts and sources in the previous chapters. Our efforts here will **not** be to marshal more facts to dispel or discredit the conventional wisdom about welfare. Rather we will seek simply to **identify** the various aspects of the myths, to likewise list the "countermyths," and to briefly discuss the issues involved. We leave to **you** the job of further research into the facts relating to these myths **and** of deciding the amount of truth they speak. In relation to each myth we will mention some possible starting points for further inquiry (see "Take-off Points," pp. 115–17).

MYTHS ABOUT WORK

There are many intertwined parts to the welfare/work myth. First, there is the idea that the only (or major) reason we have welfare is because some people are lazy and won't work. Second, there is the idea that the welfare system destroys initiative and incentive to work. It is widely believed that there are many able-bodied adults receiving welfare who could work if they just would. Many people believe, even when there is substantial unemployment, that there is a job for anyone who really wants one. Also there is widespread and uncritical acceptance of the idea that if someone on welfare does go to work he or she will be able to be self-supporting.

Countermyths about work include statistics which show that only a very small percentage of all welfare recipients are able-bodied men and women and evidence which shows that most recipients want to work.

These are the questions about welfare and work which are involved in these myths:

- Are there (or can there be created) **jobs** for those on welfare who want to work?
- What kind of **child care** will benefit children (**and** the society)? How can enough of this be made available?
- **Who should decide** whether a mother stays home to care for her children full time or goes to work?
- Should a mother (or anyone) who works always earn more money than someone who receives welfare? (The old idea of **less eligibility!**)
- Or should there be some standard of **income** as a **floor** below which we allow no one to fall? This would mean a "welfare" supplement to all who work but earn less than this floor.

MYTHS ABOUT MORALS
People talk about how welfare encourages and subsidizes or rewards immoral behavior. Most often they point to "illegitimate" (born out of wedlock) children as the evidence of this behavior. Welfare mothers are said to have more babies to get more money.

Countermyths have emerged that point to the ways in which

welfare breaks up families, and counterattacks cite abortion and illegitimacy among nonpoor people.

Men are said to desert their families so that they will be eligible for welfare and to refuse to pay child support preferring to let the government absorb the cost.

Probably if differences because of financial factors (cost of divorce for example) are taken into account the **behavior** of rich, middle, and poor people is actually remarkably similar.

In any case, key issues relating to the myths of immorality are:

1. Should welfare benefits be conditioned on certain "moral" behavior?
2. How will this behavior be judged and the standard enforced?
3. If, for example, children are to be removed from homes where a second "illegitimate" child is taken as evidence of an "unsuitable" home what will happen to these children? If the children are removed will this cost more or less than welfare? Will the threat of removal improve the morality of those so judged and treated?

MYTHS ABOUT RACE AND MIGRATION

These myths assume most people on welfare are **nonwhite** (black, Puerto Rican, or Mexican) and that they migrated (usually to cities) in order to get on welfare (or to get higher welfare payments). They also imply (or openly state) that this means that "these people" are "different" (inferior).

Countermyths point out that there are a majority of Whites on welfare and that there is no evidence that people move to get on welfare.

As with other myths statistics can be produced to buttress both sides of the argument.

Basic factors and questions bearing on this myth have to do with:

1. Should people be able to move freely about in the United States without being denied aid if they are in need?

2. What are the implications for the federal/state/local system of such mobility and of welfare grant differences between various states and localities?
3. If a higher **proportion** of people in need are of one ethnic
or minority group or another, what does it mean and
what should be done about it?

THE MYTH OF THE WELFARE CADILLAC

The import of this song (and myth) is that you can live pretty
good on welfare. A current California version talks about people with combined welfare and work incomes as high as $10,000
to $15,000.

The countermyth approach usually talks about Mississippi
grant levels, points out that many states make it impossible to
own **any** car (much less a Cadillac) and get on welfare, and
agrees that there should be some limit to welfare and work
income levels.

The issues are fairly clear:

1. How much money should people on welfare get?
2. Should some/any/all people be able to combine welfare
and work and get more than people who just work? (Less
eligibility again!)

THE MYTHS ABOUT WELFARE FRAUD

Popular belief is that most people on welfare cheat and chisel.
They conceal their Cadillacs and their boyfriends. They have
money in their mattresses and own property no one knows about.

The countermyth reminds us that a great many people cheat
on their income tax and that the welfare system is so complicated some fraud occurs out of the ignorance and/or just plain
frustration of both recipients and welfare workers.

What we need to decide is:

1. Do many people cheat? If so why and how and what can
be done about it?

2. What does it cost to **catch** cheaters versus **changing** the rule they are breaking? or just giving them **enough money** in the first place?

We hope as you have now begun to struggle with the critical issues of welfare that you find yourself somewhere in between these "old myths" and a set of "new realities." The next step is to try to gain some understanding of how these myths have been and **are still** being used in our society.

☛ DO-ITS

1. Develop a "counter-stereotype" description of an AFDC family based on the facts in chapter 3.
2. Clip out evidence of the operation of welfare stereotyping around these (or other) myths from your local newspaper and from magazines.

TAKE-OFF POINTS FOR FURTHER INQUIRY
Two recent useful "myth vs. fact" booklets are:

1. **Six Myths About Welfare**
   National Welfare Rights Organization
   1424—16th Street, N.W.
   Washington, D.C. 20036
2. **Welfare Myths vs. Facts** (SRS 71-127)
   Department of Health, Education, and Welfare
   Social and Rehabilitation Service
   Washington, D.C. 20201

Work
• "The Workfare State": A special issue on work and welfare reform. **New Generation,** 145 East 32d Street, New York, N.Y. 10016. 75¢.

- David Macarov, **Incentives to Work: The Effects of Unearned Income** (San Francisco: Jossey-Bass, Inc., 1970). An investigation of the effect that a guaranteed income would have on the work incentive of recipients.
- Dr. Leonard J. Hausman, **The Potential for Work Among Welfare Parents,** U. S. Department of Labor, Manpower Administration, Manpower Research Monograph No. 12, 1969. 45¢.
- Genevieve W. Carter, "The Employment Potential of AFDC Mothers—Some Questions and Some Answers," **Welfare in Review,** Vol. 6, No. 4, July–Aug. 1968, pp. 1–111. 35¢ GPO.
- Irene Cox, "The Employment of Mothers as a Means of Family Self Support," **Welfare in Review,** Vol. 8, No. 6, Nov.–Dec. 1970, pp. 9–17. 35¢ GPO.
- Also see Perry Levinson cited on p. 85 and Gilbert Y. Steiner cited on p. 37, especially regarding day-care issues.
- Sar A. Levitan, David Marwick, and Martin Rein, **Work and Welfare Go Together** (Baltimore: Johns Hopkins University Press, 1972). An analysis of the present welfare system and proposals for a new work-welfare plan.
- Abbie Hoffman, **Steal This Book** (also excellent regarding fraud) (New York: Pirate Edition, 1971).

Immorality
- See Phillips Cutwright, "Illegitimacy: Myths, Causes and Cures," **Family Planning Perspectives,** Vol. 3, No. 1, Jan. 1971, cited on p. 85.
- See Bell cited on p. 51.
- **Illegitimacy and Its Impact on ADC,** Bureau of Public Assistance, Washington, D.C., Apr. 1960. 35¢ GPO (a newer study may be available).
- **Illegitimacy and Dependency,** reprint from Sept. 1963 HEW Indicators.

Race and Migration
- Richard A. Cloward and Frances Fox Piven, "Migration, Politics, and Welfare," **Saturday Review,** Nov. 16, 1968, and see their **Regulating the Poor,** cited on p. 120.

THE WELFARE MYTHS

- President's Commission on Income Maintenance—Background Papers, 1969. See especially pp. 152–58.
- NWRO, "FAP and Welfare: Racist Institutions" mimeo May 11, 1971, 1424—16th St., N.W., Washington, D.C. 20036 (donation).

Welfare Cadillac
- NCSS Report AFDC-2, 1971, Part II, Financial Circumstances.

Fraud
- The Recipient Fraud Incidence Study conducted by the Fraud Review Panel for the State of California Department of Social Welfare, Jan. 1970, and Statement on the Recipient Fraud Study, Jan. 19, 1970, Social Workers' Union Local 535 SEIU, 3201 Telegraph Ave., Oakland, Calif. 94609.
- Eligibility of Families Receiving AFDC. A Report Requested by the Senate Appropriations Committee. U. S. Department of Health, Education, and Welfare, July 1963.
- Eligibility of Families Receiving AFDC in Nevada in December 1970. Department of Health, Education, and Welfare, SRS, APA, Apr. 1971.
- Report on the Disposition of Public Assistance Cases Involving Questions of Fraud, Fiscal Year 1971. NCSS Report E7 **(FY 71)**, DHEW Publication No. (SRS 72-03256).

☛ CHAPTER FIVE
THE FUNCTIONS OF WELFARE

"For the purpose of encouraging the care of dependent children . . . to help maintain and strengthen family life and to help . . . parents . . . to attain or retain capability for the maximum self support and personal independence. . . ."

> Title IV—Grants to States
> for Aid and Services to
> Needy Families with Children,
> Social Security Act.

"The public welfare program is the channel through which the Government assures each individual and family their basic living needs will be met."

> Report of the Advisory
> Council on Public Welfare,
> **Having the Power, We Have
> the Duty,** June 29, 1966.

"Historical evidence suggests that relief arrangements are initiated or expanded during the occasional outbreaks of civil disorder produced by mass unemployment, and are then abolished or contracted when political stability is restored. We shall argue that expansive relief policies are designed to mute civil disorder, and restrictive ones to reinforce work norms."

> Frances Fox Piven and
> Richard A. Cloward,
> **Regulating the Poor: The Functions of Public Relief**
> (New York: Pantheon Books, A Division of Random House, Inc., 1971).

Can the same welfare program strengthen family life, assure basic living needs, mute civil disorder, and reinforce work norms? The answer may be yes, because, as we have already seen, welfare is like an onion and an elephant—it has many layers and, like the elephant described by the blindmen, everyone sees a different part of it.

Actually there are at least three different layers of looking at welfare in our society: what it ought to do, what it does, and what we say it does.

What welfare ought to do is (or ought to be!) **our** province to decide. In a democracy the basic goals of society and governmental means of fulfilling them are supposed to be decided by the people.

It has already probably become apparent to you that there is (and has always been) a gap between what we **say** welfare does and what actually occurs. So let us try to look directly at that: How do we use welfare? and to what end? What functions does it serve?

Beatrice Webb, lecturing in 1928 on "The English Poor Law: Will It Endure?", described the function of the poor law as "summarizing the legal relations between the Haves and the Havenots."

She pointed out that up until the eighteenth century the poor law was actually called "The Law of the Poor" and in this early development had less to do with relief—with obligations of the rich to the poor—than with defining and regulating the behavior of the poor toward the rich. Mrs. Webb dubbed the result as "The Relief of Destitution Within a Framework of Repression or Charity in the Grip of Serfdom"!

So from the beginning welfare has combined "the charitable impulse" with the function of social control. Usually "charity" or the "welfare" of poor people is the publicly avowed function —what we say we are doing. For most of the people involved in administering welfare and certainly for a majority of us in whose name it is given, charity—the sincere desire to help poor people—and other such altruistic statements of purpose are not mere cover-ups for conscious "evil" intent to repress, coerce, and control. They are what we really believe.

This apparent paradox—doing good which turns out badly— is solved by William Ryan. In his recent, creative book, **Blaming the Victim,** he describes the process of "brilliant compromise" which good people use in "reconciling self interest with the promptings of humanitarian impulses."

Winifred Bell provides an AFDC case in point. Speaking of "suitable home" policies developed by many states in the 1940s and '50s, she notes:

> The evidence shows that their primary functions were (1) to restrict the growth of the caseload and (2) to inhibit ADC coverage of Negro and illegitimate children. . . . **The fact that they were widely viewed as rational measures to protect the interests and promote the welfare of children was one of their continuing assets** [boldface added].*

Any ideas that you may have had that the function of welfare is to provide for the basic living needs of children and families with no other source of income should have already been shaken

* Winifred Bell, **Aid to Dependent Children** (New York: Columbia University Press, 1965), p. 175.

by the statistics of how inadequate are the resources which we furnish.

That AFDC would not provide even minimum living needs was assured from the beginning when Congress in 1935 deleted a provision which would have required the states to provide "a reasonable subsistence compatible with decency and health." This was a **political** decision as Gilbert Steiner points out because "the provision was objectionable to Southern members of Congress who were reluctant to provide any opening wedge for federal intrusion on the handling of the Negro question." * This illustrates a welfare policy determination made in order to preserve the status quo—in this as in numerous other policy and procedural instances the particular institution involved is racism.

Frances Piven and Richard Cloward in their recent book **Regulating the Poor,** which is the **first** full study of the functions of welfare, point up an **economic** function of welfare which also should not surprise us—enforcing work norms. They make clear that they have no argument against work or against relief-giving as a mechanism to be used by society to ensure productive contributions from its members but rather with how it turns out—how welfare "defines and enforces the terms on which different classes of men are made to do different kinds of work." †

They continue, "Relief arrangements, in other words, have a great deal to do with maintaining social and economic inequities . . . and so the issue is not the relative merit of work itself; it is rather how some men are made to do the harshest work for the least reward." ‡ Welfare has always been used to force/encourage people to work. Many of its harsh, punitive, and restrictive practices can be understood in light of this func-

* Gilbert Y. Steiner, **Social Insecurity, The Politics of Welfare** (Chicago: Rand McNally & Co., 1966), p. 346.
† Frances Fox Piven and Richard Cloward, **Regulating the Poor: The Functions of Public Relief** (New York: Pantheon Books, A Division of Random House, Inc., 1971), p. xvii.
‡ Ibid.

tion. And this has also provided welfare with one of its central policy dilemmas well stated in a Washington **Post** editorial of a few years ago, "An ideal [welfare] policy ought to reward people for **staying off** relief as well as reward them for **getting off** relief" (boldface added). The dilemma is that if the reward for staying off welfare is money then that would be **welfare**! So the solution has been twofold: (1) try to make sure that welfare is less than the lowest paid employment (our old friend less eligibility) and (2) to give welfare in such a way that staying off it is the reward! As Piven and Cloward put it, "the indignities and cruelties of the dole . . . [and the] specter of ending up on 'the welfare' or in 'the poorhouse' makes any job at any wage a preferable alternative." * (For details on **how** this is done, see their chapter on the administrative methods of enforcing low-wage work [chapter 5].)

But note that "indignities and cruelties" are not **only** in terms of treatment by those who run the welfare system, whether of evil intent or do-gooders. Perhaps the most powerful of these attacks on dignity has been mounted from **within the hearts and heads of poor people themselves:** They have learned to despise themselves by absorbing the same values, work ethic, and idea the rest of us have—that being on welfare is due to personal failure. These victims blame themselves!

The role of the "Protestant work ethic" (it really is a fully ecumenical Protestant, Catholic, Jewish work ethic) in shaping these attitudes has been excellently described and analyzed by Philip Wogaman:

Whatever one may say concerning the importance of work (and I consider work to be necessary to man's personal and social fulfillment), it loses its Christian significance when it is slavery or when it is an anxious attempt to make oneself worthy. . . . In this perspective, the "Protestant ethic" (which as we have received it may be a distortion of both ethics and of Protestantism) represents a half truth. The true half is the importance of work in human fulfillment. The false

* Ibid.

half is the subordination of man to work and, worse yet, the attempt to establish whether or not people are deserving of what God has already given them.*

The "Protestant ethic," according to Wogaman, helps account for our strong emphasis on work, for the idea that it is "wrong" to be on welfare, and for the "lingering feeling that prosperous people generally have more character and moral fiber than the poor." From these ideas it is easy to conclude that the poor are to blame for poverty and that they deserve it **and** the welfare system.

If at this point your reaction is defensive, please pause and reflect. No one is attacking **you** with these ideas.

Rather this discussion is simply intended as a small and tentative step toward helping **us** see the world (and welfare) as it is. But this can be both painful and "dangerous." For, as previously mentioned, if there is any "conspiracy" involved in welfare it is that these kinds of underlying political and economic aspects which shape its role in our society are not to be discussed. We will chance it by briefly exploring the economics and politics of welfare, seeking to suggest the possibilities rather than state conclusions. However, before we begin work on a political and economic analysis of the welfare system let us look at its present **legal** status.

THE "LAW" OF WELFARE
Welfare law has a fascinating history. Law mirrors society. The legal status of an institution reflects its social situation.

One of the first and most important people to look at the law of welfare in our time was a remarkable man named Jacobus tenBroek.

A blindman, constitutional lawyer, professor of political science, chairman of the California State Social Welfare Board, and organizer/founder of the National Federation of the Blind, tenBroek in the early 1950s "rediscovered" the law of the poor

* Philip Wogaman, **Guaranteed Annual Income, The Moral Issues** (Nashville: Abingdon Press, 1968). Used by permission.

and began to study and write about it, especially about welfare law as a part of what he came to call the "dual system of law" —one for the poor and one for the rest of society. Today's "poverty lawyers" are tenBroek's direct heirs.

Elizabeth Wickenden became interested in these issues and ideas in the early 1960s. She wrote a memorandum in 1963 titled "The Constitutional Rights of Assistance Recipients" in which she observed that "many critics of the contemporary social scene . . . have recently expressed their concern over the mounting evidence that poverty itself constitutes a barrier to equal treatment under law." **Note:** Even this state of affairs is an improvement over the earlier idea that to be poor is a crime in itself.

In 1965 Charles Reich (of current **Greening of America** fame) wrote in the **Yale Law Journal,** "The time has come for lawyers to take a major interest in social welfare."

He listed some of the issues as regulations which attempt to impose a standard of moral behavior on recipients, investigations, searches, and "midnight raids," residence, and whether a recipient must work to obtain aid and what work he may be compelled to do. He identified questions of law underlying these issues: administrative and procedural questions, constitutional questions relating to personal liberty, due process, and equal protection, and the key question of entitlement—the right to welfare.

In the 1960s a group of lawyers arose and began to seek answers to these questions. Under our legal system answers to questions like these must come out of "fighting them out" in court. "Justice" too is a function of this adversary process. And to get justice in America you need a lawyer. Welfare recipients finally got some lawyers, so they **began** to get some justice.

A detailed discussion of the exciting development in welfare law during the last ten years is not possible here. It is, however, a story which needs to be told. Here we can only mention a few highlights.

In 1969 the U. S. Supreme Court struck down AFDC residence

requirements as violating the constitutional right of movement and travel. This case was remarkable because it represented the first time in the more than thirty-year history of the AFDC program that a welfare recipient had been able to get a lawyer and get into a federal court on a constitutional issue!

A series of court cases successfully attacked many of the issues raised by tenBroek, Reich, Wickenden, and others, and suddenly welfare recipients found that they had rights. And much of this was made possible with **government** money!—despite the feeling and opposition of public officials like Senator Russell Long who has observed about the government-sponsored neighborhood legal services, "Nobody in his right mind would hire a lawyer to file a lawsuit against himself."

None of these issues in themselves were as important as the key underlying issue of the **right to welfare.** Most Americans would agree that welfare recipients should have the same constitutional rights as everyone else. However, far fewer think of welfare as a right. We may not want to go as far as Thomas Malthus, the English economist and clergyman, who argued that any "right to subsistence" goes against the laws of nature, but are we willing to accept Reich's formulation: "When individuals have insufficient resources to live under conditions of health and decency, society has obligations to provide support, and the individual is entitled to that support as [a] right"?

Edward V. Sparer, regarded by most of us welfare "lawyers" as our leader (I cheerfully admit to practicing welfare law without a license), has put the question in its most compelling form, "Is there a constitutional right to live?"

In the 1960s, for a time it appeared that the courts (and the public) might be moving toward acceptance of this truly radical notion—a right to live. But repression has set in and in our concern for "law and order" there does not appear to be room for a right to live.

The Burger Court in one of its first decisions overruled the lower courts in upholding the state of Maryland's maximum AFDC grant system. That decision (in **Dandridge** v. **Williams**) talked in terms of the state's right to regulate in the social and economic field. In citing business and industry cases in support of unequal treatment if the classification involved has some "reasonable basis," the majority opinion held that: "The administration of public welfare assistance, by contrast, involves the most basic economic needs of impoverished human beings. We recognize the dramatically real factual difference between the cited cases and this one, but **we can find no basis for applying a different constitutional standard**" (boldface added).

This decision may some day take its place with the Dred Scott case which upheld the doctrine that Negroes "had no rights or privileges but such as those who held the power and the Government might choose to grant them." (Roger Rice called this parallel to my attention.)

In any case, for the time being welfare recipients may have some rights but not **economic** rights and not the right to live. Oh well, such, as Robert M. O'Neil puts it in the title of his book, is "the price of dependency." Will the lawyers win, will the recipients get their rights? Stay tuned for more developments in law of welfare!

The Right to Live

There are American poor, in and out of "welfare," who refuse to tolerate starvation conditions on the ground that neither Constitution nor statute nor court decision appears to impose upon our government an obligation to protect all of its citizens against starvation. There are also large numbers of Americans, apparently drawn from various classes, who would cast such folk outside the pale of constitutional protection and withdraw all their rights.

It is argued that the Constitution is designed to assure democratic results: the majority governs through the elective process; the minority is guaranteed the right to dissent. Those are the ground rules by which all members of the American society must abide. These rules are subject today to increasing challenge. Upon what moral premise must the starving man or woman accept the majority's vote on whether he or she shall live or not? What moral premise requires that the youth accept the majority's vote on whether he must kill other men? What moral premise requires that the black man accept the results of the white majority vote on whether obstacles to his equality shall be removed?

The persuasive argument on such issues has not been moral, but pragmatic: If you do not accept these ground rules, the result will be chaos. To which some who suffer under such ground rules, and their sympathizers, reply: We do not prefer the status quo to chaos; only the relatively comfortable see the issue of change in such terms. The ground rules must do more than guarantee the right to persuade the majority, they must guarantee the right to live, whatever the majority thinks. The right to live is a sine qua non of the social contract.

IF IT IS NOT IN PRESENT LAW AND CONSTITUTION THEN WHAT?

Source: Edward V. Sparer, "The Illegality of Poverty," *Social Policy,* Mar.–Apr. 1971, pp. 49–50. Republished in *The Rights of Americans,* ed. Norman Dorsen. Copyright © 1970, 1971 by Random House, Inc. Used by permission of Pantheon Books/A Division of Random House, Inc.

THE REASON *WE* NEED A CONSTITUTION . . .

Is there a constitutional right to "adequate" welfare payments? The courts have given no answer, and most likely will give none for the foreseeable future. Professor Edward Sparer of the University of Pennsylvania argues, however, that a constitutional "right to live" is implicit in other liberties that courts traditionally recognize and protect. "The guarantee of life," he maintains, "is as essential as the right to dissent, as essential as the guarantee of free speech or the free exercise of religion." Indeed, he adds that the traditional liberties cannot survive without recognition of a right of subsistence: "Let the unemployed man lie starving, let the sick woman die because an affluent society won't provide her with minimal medical treatment, and you have killed off the speaker, the writer and the worshipper. You have preserved these rights only for the comfortable and the affluent. The reason we need a constitution is to protect the rights of the weak, the powerless and the dispossessed."

Although most constitutional scholars still reject so sweeping a claim to public assistance, Sparer points to a recent decision by three federal judges in New York. Acknowledging that "welfare benefits may not at the present time constitute the exercise of a constitutional right," the court found "basic concepts of humanity and decency" implicit in the "general welfare" clause of the Constitution. One of those concepts "is the desire to ensure that indigent, unemployable citizens will at least have the bare minimums required for existence, without which our expressed fundamental constitutional rights and liberties frequently cannot be exercised and therefore become meaningless."

Is to Preserve Our Rights

Source: From the book *The Price of Dependency: Civil Liberties in the Welfare State* by Robert M. O'Neil. Copyright © 1970 by Robert M. O'Neil. Published by E. P. Dutton & Co., Inc. and used with their permission.

THE ECONOMICS OF WELFARE

As we have seen, total federal, state, and local welfare spending is now approaching $18 billion a year. Yet, there are very few studies of the economic impact of this spending. In fact, more seems to be written nowadays about the **possible** effects of various "guaranteed income" schemes than on the **actual** present role of public assistance in our economy.

Income in the traditional economic view is the source of consumption. In a consumer-based economy, in a consumption-oriented society, why hasn't more attention been paid to the role of welfare in making it possible for poor people to continue fulfilling the consumer's role?

Isn't it in fact likely that with continued technological "progress" poor people (and indeed all of us!) may be more and more needed as consumers and less and less needed as "producers"?

A science fiction story by Frederik Pohl pursues this possibility into a future in which rich people enjoy the privilege of leading a spare and spartan life while the poor are forced to consume, consume, consume—or else. And while that may strike you as extreme, what about congressional testimony of farmer groups in support of food stamps because they strengthen the **corn** market—you see food stamps enable recipients to buy a little more meat, and meat is produced by feeding **corn** to **cattle.** I was there to hear that testimony and, in the time-honored tradition of free enterprise, thought immediately of making the system work more efficiently by simply eliminating the middle man—the cattle. We could feed the corn **directly** to the poor and even eliminate the food stamps too! If you are unwilling to entertain this idea at least you will agree that food stamps are an excellent example of how welfare may be used to control behavior—in this case **economic** behavior. The way food stamps work is that in return for a little more aid (in the form of the food stamp bonus) recipients must give up freedom to spend that aid as they might wish and instead are required to spend it (as a condition for getting the "extra") on what we want them to (food in this case). And, that behavior is **designed** to economically aid someone else (here the farmer and food distributor). No wonder the same farmers' organization also testified at this hearing in favor of "cotton stamps."

In any case, some effort to trace the cost flow and economic implications for local communities, states, and the nation of increased (or decreased) welfare payments seems in order. If all the welfare recipients in a small town were to mark their dollars with a red W before they spent them, they might be able to show people just who profits from welfare and where the taxpayers' money goes! (We understand a similar device for "explaining" the relevant economics has been employed by the armed services by using two-dollar bills to pay servicemen when tension about their presence arises in local communities with large military installations.)

With the high ratio of federal to state and local dollars in welfare in many poor states (especially in the South—almost 80 percent of Mississippi's welfare payments is federal money) it even has been estimated that because of a multiplier effect (each dollar is in effect spent several times) some states may actually **make money** on welfare in that the small number of state dollars required to bring large numbers of federal dollars into the state may be more than offset by the income to the state from the sales taxes and income taxes generated by the consumer spending resulting from welfare grants.

Of course, in order for this idea to be used as an argument to **raise** grants, there must be willingness to deal with other implications of increasing welfare grants. In the South, welfare has always been used as a weapon to sustain segregation and most recently, to attempt to force Blacks to leave the South because they are no longer needed economically (to chop and pick cotton for example) and because they are a growing political threat to those who hold power. This is illustrated in the shift from surplus commodity programs to food stamp programs toward the end of the 1960s. Food stamps require cash to participate and interpose new bureaucratic barriers as well. This "southern strategy" combines economic and political uses of welfare. Economically welfare is used to insure an adequate low wage labor supply **and** to insure that people work when needed—in Mississippi (and in other states, such as California, which use farm labor) welfare administration relaxes in the winter and pushes people off welfare as needed in the fields in the spring and summer.

Irene Lurie, in the only study of the economics of AFDC I could find, makes the important economic point that AFDC payments should not only be viewed as short-run transfer payments helping reduce **present** poverty through increasing consumption but as **investment** by virtue of their potential for raising the productivity of recipients in the future. We should, she argues, view AFDC as an investment in human beings.

This discussion of the economic functions of welfare could continue but with these few admittedly sketchy illustrations, we simply assert that it is time we **knew** more and move on to the politics of welfare.

THE POLITICS OF WELFARE
Again we must begin by pointing up the dismal state of our information. There has been little work on how welfare is used politically. That it **is** used politically, we think no one will dispute. With the leading politicians of the nation using the welfare issue in a variety of ways, most people have some general sense that welfare is a political issue. However, there has been little done to make explicit just **how** welfare is used politically. Here are some examples:

1. **As a scapegoat and distraction**—to take people's minds off where money really goes and to confuse the priority choices. In California, for example, Governor Reagan has been using welfare in this way to avoid tax reform which could be at the expense of his business constituency.
2. **As a wedge to keep various groups divided politically**—most notably in the continued pitting of the "working poor" against the "welfare poor" keeping them from building political alliances to move on the basis of their substantial common self-interest. This particular divide-and-rule situation is threatened by wage supplements. The working poor may figure out that wage supplements, "work incentives," Family Assistance payments, even Medicaid are **welfare.** It may become as important to see to it that the working poor get more money than welfare recipients so they will continue to see themselves and their interests as **different** from welfare recipients as it has been as a "carrot" to keep them working.
3. **To "purchase" and/or to reward constituencies** (and thus to build new constituencies). By this, I mean something more sophisticated than the allegation that it is easier to get on welfare in Chicago if you are part of (or go via) the

Daley machine. Haven't President Nixon and Congressman Wilbur Mills, chairman of the House Ways and Means Committee, been trying to do some of this with the current welfare reform proposals? A simple-minded version of it could work like this. A working poor family suddenly receives a FAP supplement to their meager earnings. They are pleased and grateful. Whom do they vote for: Nixon or Wallace?—unless Mills runs too! (See following chapter on welfare reform for a more detailed discussion of the politics of Family Assistance.)

Of course, politics is not all that simple. Working people may resent being put "on welfare." They might even take the money and vote for Reagan who seems to be using the welfare issue to put together and communicate with a slightly different constituency; a suburban/rural anti-central city coalition. Gov. Nelson Rockefeller of New York has used welfare in this way **and** at the same time gotten antiwelfare working class, ethnic votes in the city. In any case, the point is that welfare can be used as an element in constructing political constituencies.

4. **To avert the threat of political disruption.** Here Piven and Cloward have again done almost the only systematic work. Their thesis is that welfare is applied to cool-out people when they make political "noise." They describe this as "dissensus" politics. If a group poses a "dissensus" threat, that is, to pull out of somebody's "consensus," the response is to attempt to keep them in by granting concessions. This, Piven and Cloward argue, is what happened in the case of Blacks and the Democrats in the 1960s. The civil rights movement in the South and the riots in northern ghettos made Blacks a political threat to the Democratic consensus. Welfare programs, including the War on Poverty but especially easier access to the AFDC rolls in the cities, were the political response to this threat.

5. **As communication, particularly as symbolic communication** —an example of this would be using welfare as a code word to stir up and evoke racial hostilities. This is part of the

"how" of divide and rule. Antiwelfare talk and proposals help keep middle- and lower-income Whites and even other emerging poor groups such as Puerto Ricans and Mexican-Americans politically separate and competing with rather than politically coalescing with Blacks.

Another example of such symbolic use of welfare is to tap and play on antibig government, antibureaucracy sentiments. Both President Nixon and Governor Reagan have combined this with an additional political strategy in their talk of returning government and power to "the people." They both are talking about the same people—Republicans.

It is no accident that Republican welfare reform provisions would fiscally benefit governmental units where there is the most Republican political power—states and counties. Democrats have been more interested in by-passing the states to deal directly with the cities, which they usually control.

No summary of the politics of welfare would be complete without mention of the most exciting new element in the welfare and indeed, I believe, in the national political process in our times. The emergence of the National Welfare Rights Organization in the past five years has changed the entire welfare situation. (The welfare rights movement is entitled to their own book. My own deep personal involvement with NWRO has made it **very** difficult to write just these few paragraphs!)*

For the first time (at least in the AFDC program) welfare recipients are organized, speaking, and taking action in their own behalf. This kind of political participation is not only important to the recipients but it is vital to the rest of us as well. The U. S. Court of Appeals, in affirming NWRO's right to participate in an HEW hearing, took note of this: "As intervenors in conformity hearings [organized welfare recipients] may serve the **public interest**" (boldface added).

Sparer has argued that many of welfare's inadequacies and inequalities can be explained by the fact that it has always been

* For additional information, see pages 139—41.

we who have decided what would be good for **them,** we who "benevolently" set the structures, policies, and practices. Now, in welfare we are on the threshold of the kind of improvements industry experienced when labor organized in the 1930s. When someone you have power over begins to redress that imbalance, first you say that it won't work, then afterward you are surprised how much it benefits **you**! And, if anyone tries to tell you that it is un-American for people receiving government benefits to organize and lobby, tell them about the American Legion and veterans' pensions.*

Again, we could go on. Again, no matter what further questions you may want to raise about these particular examples, we are on the right track of beginning to educate ourselves to the creative political possibilities of welfare.

A SHORT SUMMARY
Welfare did not just happen. It has grown because it serves useful functions in our society. However, it is safe to say mildly that welfare has not been an instrument of positive progress toward social justice! Perhaps even more serious has been the fact that its functions have not been known, understood, analyzed, and discussed. Welfare has an economics. It has a politics. If there is to be progress we must begin to understand how welfare works in these ways—what its role in our society is. Then with a clear understanding for what is **and** of the creative possibilities available to us we can go forward to make welfare do what we want it to. But before we turn to those possibilities and how to work toward making them happen, we must take a step backward and talk about welfare reform.

☛ **DO-ITS**
1. **Clip the newspaper and watch television for examples of political and economic uses of welfare.**

* See Gilbert Y. Steiner, **The State of Welfare** (Washington: The Brookings Institution, 1971), chap. 7.

2. Talk with a lawyer at your city's neighborhood legal services program for information on current welfare law cases in your state.
3. Armed with facts about welfare expenditures in your area, survey local businessmen to see if they are aware of this money flow. Food stores are a good starting point.
4. Read Frances Fox Piven and Richard A. Cloward, Regulating the Poor: The Functions of Public Relief (New York: Pantheon, 1971; available as a Vintage Press paperback, $2.45). Be clear on your agreements and disagreements with this book. It will likely dominate the discussion of the economics and politics of welfare for some time.
5. To delve further into the fascinating subject of welfare law try
   • Robert M. O'Neil, The Price of Dependency: Civil Liberties in the Welfare State (New York: E. P. Dutton & Co., 1970).
   • Jacobus tenBroek, ed., The Law of the Poor (San Francisco: Chandler Publishing Company, 1966). A collection of articles from a conference.
   • Edward V. Sparer in Norman Dorsen, ed., The Rights of Americans: What They Are—What They Should Be (New York: Pantheon, 1971).
6. There has been very little written on the economics of the present welfare system. For the only study of the economics of AFDC that I could find, see Irene Lurie, An Economic Evaluation of AFDC (Washington: The Brookings Institution, 1968).
7. Gilbert Y. Steiner's first welfare book, Social Insecurity, The Politics of Welfare (Chicago: Rand McNally & Co., 1966) opens up many of the key policy and political issues.
8. And for a glimpse of consumerism extended to its logical extreme read Frederik Pohl, "The Midas Plague," The Case Against Tomorrow (New York: Ballantine Books, 1957, 1965).

THESE ARE THE RIGHTS

Bill of Welfare Rights

1   The right to be a member of a Welfare Rights Organization.
2   The right to fair and equal treatment, free from discrimination based on race, color or religion.
3   The right to apply for any welfare program and to have that application put in writing.
4   The right to have the welfare department make a decision promptly after application for aid.
5   The right to be told in writing the specific reason for any denial of aid.
6   The right to a hearing *before* your check can be reduced or cut off and before your medical aid is affected.
7   The right to appeal a denial of aid and to be given a *fair hearing* before an impartial referee.
8   The right to get welfare payments without being forced to spend the money as the welfare department wants.
9   The right to be treated with respect.
10 The right to be treated in a way which does not invade your privacy.
11 The right to receive welfare aid without having the welfare department ask you questions about who your social friends are (such as who you are going out with).
12 The right to have the same constitutional protections that all other citizens have.
13 The right to be told and informed by the welfare department of all of your rights, including the ways you can best make sure that you can get your welfare money.
14 The right to have, to get, and to give advice during all contacts with the welfare department, including when applying, when being investigated, and during fair hearings.

THAT THE WELFARE RIGHTS MOVEMENT IS ABOUT!

Source: Reprinted by permission of
National Welfare Rights Organization.

WELFARE IN COURT
By Fred P. Graham*

WASHINGTON—Despite the time-honored admonitions that one should not bite the hand that feeds him nor look a gift horse in the mouth, welfare clients are suddenly suing welfare officials at a record clip.

Until two years ago, it was virtually unknown for a person on welfare to sue the officials who were paying for his bed and board. But since that time, in a number of test cases that have been brought in courts across the country, welfare recipients have challenged the way in which they are being treated by those who sign their relief checks.

Several forces appear to have triggered this burst of litigation: the attention that the "war on poverty" focused on the plight of the poor, the availability of Federal funds to pay lawyers for poor people, and the creation of legal research units that specialize in welfare law—notably welfare law centers at Columbia and New York Universities.

Request for Stay

The results were apparent last week when Alabama authorities asked Supreme Court Justice Hugo L. Black to stay a lower court decision that had declared unconstitutional the state's controversial "substitute father" welfare rule.

This regulation—and similar ones in 18 other states—denies welfare benefits to the children of women who engage in extra-marital sexual relations, on the theory that any man who enjoys such domestic privileges should pay the household bills.

By invoking this rule, Alabama had cut its aid to dependent children lists by almost one-fourth in three years. Now that a court has ruled that the state cannot punish the children for the sins of the parents, the state claims that it cannot meet its other welfare obligations.

* **The New York Times,** November 26, 1967. © 1967 by The New York Times Company. Reprinted by permission.

THE FUNCTIONS OF WELFARE

It is appealing to the Supreme Court, in the first high Court test of the "substitute father" rule.

A number of other welfare test cases are now before lower courts and are certain to be appealed to the Supreme Court, regardless of which side wins.

Test Cases

They include a claim that a welfare recipient must be given a hearing before benefits are revoked, a charge that mothers of young children on relief cannot be forced to accept full-time work, suits that challenge the right of welfare workers to pry into clients' premises and private lives, and a case that questions the right of welfare officials to make a welfare client pay back the amount of his benefits if he ever becomes solvent.

Taken together, these and other pending cases assert a "bill of rights" for welfare clients.

The theory is that although the Constitution does not require that the Government provide welfare, once a system is established, clients have a right to receive their benefits without interruption except for good cause and after a fair hearing, free of intrusion by welfare officials into their private lives, and without discrimination.

These are novel assertions, and as the shibboleths of American folklore suggest, are alien to the national traditions of self-reliance and free enterprise.

Yet the clients are winning almost all of their cases in the lower courts—perhaps because there are no precedents to bind the judges —and it is already apparent that, barring a stunning series of reversals in the Supreme Court, the welfare clients' "bill of rights" will be transformed from a theory to a fact in a few years.

ALL ABOUT NWRO*

The National Welfare Rights Organization is an organization of welfare recipients and other low income people, linked up in

* Reprinted by permission of National Welfare Rights Organization.

local groups, with the goals of Adequate Income, Dignity, Justice and Democracy.

NWRO is a membership organization. There are approximately 125,000 dues-paying members in 800 local groups in 50 states. NWRO is poor people . . . black, white, Chicano, Puerto Rican and Indian . . . speaking for themselves and fighting for a fair share of America.

The goal: Jobs or Income Now! Decent jobs with adequate pay for those who can work. Adequate Income for those who cannot. We demand a minimum of $6500 (at 1971 prices) for a family of four . . . from welfare or wages.

 Our symbol, the link, represents a chain of poor people linked together in the common struggle for the right to live. It symbolizes our dedication to the goals of Adequate Income, Dignity, Justice and Democracy for all people.

HISTORY OF NWRO . . .

In June, 1966, Ohio welfare recipients held a 150 mile "walk for decent welfare" from Cleveland to the state capital, Columbus. As the mothers reached Columbus on June 30th, recipient groups from Boston, Massachusetts to San Bernardino, California staged demonstrations at their welfare departments. Across the country recipients joined to support the Ohio demands, while protesting their own welfare problems. A new movement was born . . . the National Welfare Rights Movement.

More than 100 recipients attended the first national meeting in August, 1966. A National Coordinating Committee was set up. A newsletter began publication and a membership system was established. On June 30th, 1967, more than 5,000 recipients, in 40 cities, demonstrated under the banner of the National Welfare Rights Movement.

Representatives from 73 WROs met in August, 1967, and formed the National Welfare Rights Organization . . . the first

THE FUNCTIONS OF WELFARE

nationwide membership organization of poor people since the 1930s. A constitution was written, officers elected and goals adopted. Since then, NWRO has become the major national spokesman for poor people and has adopted the specific goal of $6500 Guaranteed Adequate Income for every family of four.

HOW NWRO IS SUPPORTED . . .

Members of WROs pay $1 a year dues to NWRO and most groups have local dues. But NWRO and local groups must also rely on contributions from private individuals, churches, unions, foundations, and others as a source of financial support.

Individuals whose earnings are above the NWRO Adequate Income level may become Friends of Welfare Rights by contributing $10 or more to the local and National Welfare Rights Organization. In some areas, Friends of Welfare Rights have formed organizations to raise money and support Welfare Rights in other ways. The National Office sends every Friend a subscription to THE WELFARE FIGHTER, a Friends button, and other information about NWRO.

HOW CAN YOU GET INFORMATION???

Contact the National Welfare Rights Organization

1424–16th Street, N.W.
Washington, D.C. 20036
(202)483–1531

☞ CHAPTER SIX
WELFARE REFORM

WHAT IS WELFARE REFORM ABOUT?
We have had welfare "crisis," welfare "mess," and welfare "reform" with us at least as long as welfare. Welfare reform has been happening regularly in this country ever since our **present** welfare system was established in 1935 and, of course, before that from the beginning of the "modern" welfare system in medieval times in Europe and England and since we brought it to America with us as colonists.

Whether in England in 1834 or 1909, in Newburgh, New York in 1961, (see Do-its on p. 158 for more on Newburgh), or in California, Nevada, New York (and other states) in 1971 and 1972, the rhetoric and proposals of welfare crisis and welfare reform have had similar elements.

As we have just seen in chapter 5, this is no coincidence. It results from the functions of welfare: the economic and political uses of welfare in society.

The "themes" of welfare crisis and reform are as simple as one, two, three and A, B, C:

1. A.   there are too many people on welfare,
    B.   too many of them (most) are undeserving,
    C.   more people are getting on (rolls are rising).

This is a crisis because

2. A. they get too much money,
   B. it costs the taxpayers too much,
   C. it threatens to bankrupt our government.

The reason for it is

3. A. they won't work;
   B. they cheat, chisel and defraud;
   C. they have "illegitimate" children (because of immoral behavior).

And given this analysis of "crisis" the "solutions" are equally simple:

1. A. force them to work,
   B. or starve (cut them off),
   C. if no jobs—make work.
2. A. make it hard to get on,
   B. make it harder to stay on,
   C. make it impossible to cheat.
3. A. find their relatives and make them pay (especially absent fathers),
   B. find another level of government and make **them** pay,
   C. make welfare recipients themselves pay if the rolls keep rising by cutting aid and spending the same (or **less**) money on more people.

If you programmed these "themes" into a computer—or gave them written on small pieces of paper to a group of monkeys to arrange—you could come up with all the get-tough-on-welfare speeches and most of the "welfare study commission" reports about welfare reform for the past two hundred years.

ANOTHER WELFARE REFORM STRATEGY

It has been impressed upon us in the course of our enquiry that the name "Poor Law" has gathered about it associations of harshness, and still more of hopelessness, which we fear might seriously obstruct the reforms which we desire to see initiated. We are aware that a mere change of name will not prevent the old associations from recurring, if it does not represent an essential change in the spirit of the work. But in our criticism and recommendations we hope to show the way to a system of help which will be better expressed by the title of Public Assistance than by that of Poor Law.

Source: Majority Report, 1909,
Poor Law Commission (England).

Alms
Charity
Poor Law
Public Assistance
Public Welfare
Social Services
Income Maintenance
Family Assistance Program
Opportunities for Families
Guaranteed Annual Income

At least change the name.

Welfare reform does have one possibly unique element. It is the only "reform" where there is a clear attack on the victims of the institution involved. This is related to but somewhat different from the blaming-the-victim approach described by William Ryan.

Usually, no matter with what vigor we attack the institution —"progressive" education, "foreign" aid, the prison system, for example—we do not attack the victims of that system, nor do we expect them to change **before** we change the policies involved. (An exception to this which well illustrates the point and proves the rule was the classic statement of Lester Maddox, former governor of Georgia, that he could not improve the situation in Georgia's prisons further unless they had a better class of prisoner.)

WELFARE REFORM   145

Actually—and it may be truer than we suspect—we view **ourselves** as the "victims" of welfare, not the recipients. **They** are viewed as the cause, so attacking them **is** an effort to get at the root causes of the problem!

The usual sequence welfare reform follows is familiar: (1) **political attack,** which is used to stir up; (2) **public outrage** to which officials then respond by; (3) **appointing a commission,** which studies the problem and produces; (4) **a learned report,** summarizing the history of the problem, pointing out its complex nature, and proposing several simple reforms which are then; (5) **accepted** if they are tough enough **and**/or **attacked** as too lenient; (6) then some new programs, policies, procedures are **launched with fanfare;** and, finally (7) the whole thing is **forgotten** until the next welfare reform sequence begins.

WHAT ARE THE GENERAL RESULTS OF WELFARE REFORM?

First of all, few welfare recipients ever get jobs from it. (There are few jobs available to them in the first place, and relatively few **can** work. The training, child care, and medical services necessary to make it possible for mothers to work are unavailable and expensive to develop.) Second, those who are forced off welfare must starve, double up with relatives, or just barely survive until they either get some work or, as is often the case, get back on welfare. (In the recent illegal "purge" of the rolls in Nevada many of those cut off appear to have moved to California.) Third, most of the "reforms" talked about (or even actually **legislated**) are never put into effect largely because they are very expensive, uneconomical, and much easier to talk about than to carry out. Efforts to track down and squeeze out support from absent low-income fathers, creation of public work projects, and other such measures start big and disappear quickly.

WHY THEN DO WE KEEP HAVING WELFARE CRISES AND WELFARE REFORM?

Because, as we already learned, it is part of how welfare fulfills economic and political functions in our society! With welfare readily available to those that Daniel Moynihan has described as "minor figures seeking to make an impact on the public" and its proven ability as a scapegoat for all the fiscal ills of state and local government, it is a wonder why we don't have **more** "welfare reform"!

Welfare reform, argue Piven and Cloward, is inevitable. It is an integral part of the "cycle of relief giving." First comes unemployment, then rising discontent among the poor, then expansion of welfare to cool out conflict and restore order, and **then** comes "welfare reform"—forcing persons who got on welfare during this expansion back to work. Welfare reform in this "restrictive" phase of the cycle often first takes the form of **"work"** relief (versus "direct" relief) even though this costs money **and** in the short run may **increase** the number of persons on welfare. The reasons for this are that it is the reestablishment of social control and the work "ethic" which is the goal— not just putting people off welfare—which might just lead to more turmoil. Piven and Cloward illustrate their thesis with the example of the Great Depression when rising unemployment led to rising discontent which was met at first with direct relief (Federal Emergency Relief), then as order was restored there was a shift to work relief (WPA) which in 1935 got large numbers of Americans off relief but also got many on—on WPA, PWA, CCC—the work relief programs of the depression—then were phased out gradually leaving people to fend for themselves in the labor market. What happened to these people and what would have happened to more if the true welfare reform program of that era—World War II—with its attendant full employment had not come along, we do not know.

If Piven and Cloward are right, how does their argument apply to today's welfare reforms? Well, we have had the unemployment of postwar recessions and the turmoil of the civil rights movement, and ghetto rebellions of the 1960s. And we have had the expansion of the welfare rolls.

Now it is time again for "welfare reform"! And, as we shall see, the Nixon-Mills welfare reform is **work**-oriented.

But before we examine the Nixon welfare reform proposals

let us again underline one important thing. Although our style and sense of humor may have raised your hackles (particularly if you are a "foe") and although our exposition of the Piven and Cloward thesis and our simplification of welfare reform may turn you off, don't **either** just grudgingly take our word for it **or** reject these ideas because we did not make a good enough case for them. Look at welfare reform history **for yourself.** Decide **for yourself** why (or indeed whether) these themes have occurred again and again. And remember, saying welfare has economic and political functions is **not** the same as saying that that is an "evil conspiracy" conducted by a shadowy few under the cover of our humanitarian impulses. The truth may lie somewhere in between and must be found by getting out and looking for it!

THE NIXON-MILLS WELFARE REFORM PLAN
The work-oriented phase of current welfare reform actually began in 1967. Foreshadowed by a small community work and training program authorized in 1962 as a result of the Newburgh outcry and by the Title V Work Experience Program of the Economic Opportunity Act, Congress created the Work Incentive Program (called WIN because of the obvious bad image of WIP).

The services/rehabilitate-people-off-welfare approach had failed. The rolls had continued to grow. President Lyndon B. Johnson recommended modest improvements of the welfare system, but Congressman Wilbur Mills had a better idea. Dubbed the "antiwelfare" law by the newly emerging welfare rights movement, Chairman Mills mixed work relief with a get-tough approach on illegitimacy procedures, added a fail-safe provision called the welfare freeze, and the 1967 Social Security amendments were underway.

In the Senate, Russell B. Long, son of Huey, was not about to "share the wealth," as his father had advocated. Of NWRO welfare recipient leaders who in a historic first came to testify **in their own behalf,** he said, "If they can find time to march in the streets, picket, and sit all day in Committee hearing rooms, they can find time to do some useful work. They could be picking up litter in front of their houses or killing rats instead of impeding the work of Congress."

The NWRO mothers staged what the papers called a "wait-in" or an "anger-in" in the Finance Committee Hearing room. Senator Long called them a "bunch of brood mares." Most liberals decided that welfare recipients had hurt their own cause with such militant tactics and later blamed NWRO for the negative provisions of the amendments.

On the Senate floor, there was a liberal-led fight to temper the toughness with mercy by softening the work requirements. Much to the amazement of the "old pro" welfare lobbyists, the liberals won several of their points. Senators Fred Harris (Dem.-Okla.) and Robert F. Kennedy (Dem.-N.Y.) led the fight. Kennedy said, "The House proposals seem to punish the poor because they are there and we have not been able to do anything about them. But if this is our approach, they will still be there when we are done. And the problem will be no closer to solution."

He showed limited understanding of the real idea of welfare reform but was clear about the amendments in this comment: "Public money might be saved but only because people badly in need of assistance would be eliminated from the welfare rolls without having anywhere else to turn."

After the liberal concessions were won in the Senate, the bill went to the conference committee where Mills and Long simply agreed to revert for the most part to Mills's original version.

Kennedy threatened to filibuster against the bill but Long calmly outmaneuvered him and the "antiwelfare bill" was sent to President Johnson.

Walter Reuther, speaking for organized labor, urged President Johnson to veto it calling it "a bad bill [which] cannot be defended on either economic or moral grounds." But President Johnson, even though mentioning "certain severe restrictions" and directing HEW to work with the states "so that compassionate safeguards are established to protect deserving mothers and needy children," signed it into law in January 1968. **And** he created another commission to look into "any and every proposal however unconventional, which could promise a constructive advance in meeting the income needs of all the American people."

Actually, it was a "constructive advance" that had already begun to happen which was to provide much of the element of "compassionate safeguard" of which the President spoke. For far from hurting their own cause, newly organized welfare recipients continued exposing the law's "attack on poor people," educating welfare recipients on their rights, and pressing both HEW and the Department of Labor for regulations to protect recipients from "literal" interpretation of the law's provisions.

And so, the "antiwelfare law" failed, the rolls continued to climb and in Gilbert Steiner's phrase we got "new men" to deal with the "old data."

President Nixon, after a period of policy-making that included internal jockeying for position by those advising him on welfare —Daniel Moynihan, Robert Finch, George Schultz, Arthur Burns, John Ehrlichman and Richard Nathan—addressed himself to the job of welfare reform on nationwide radio and television on August 8, 1969:

Whether measured by the anguish of the poor themselves, or by the drastically mounting burden on the taxpayer, the present welfare system has to be judged a colossal failure. Our states and cities find themselves sinking in a welfare quagmire, as caseloads increase, as costs escalate, and as the welfare system stagnates enterprise and perpetuates dependency. What began on a small scale in the depression thirties has become a monster in the prosperous sixties. The tragedy is not only that it is bringing states and cities to the brink of financial disaster, but also that it is failing to meet the elementary human, social, and financial needs of the poor. It breaks up homes. It often penalizes work. It robs recipients of dignity. And it grows.

He made some startling proposals:

> I propose that we abolish the present welfare system and adopt in its place a new family assistance system. Initially, this new system would cost more than welfare. But unlike welfare, it is designed to correct the condition it deals with and thus to lessen the long-range burden.
>
> But the program now called "Aid to Families with Dependent Children"—the program we normally think of when we think of "welfare"—would be done away with completely. The new family assistance system I propose in its place rests essentially on three principles: equality of treatment, a work requirement, and a work incentive.
>
> Its benefits would go to the working poor, as well as the nonworking; to families with dependent children headed by a father, as well as to those headed by a mother; and a basic Federal minimum would be provided, the same in every state.
>
> I propose that the Federal government build a foundation under the income of every American family with dependent children that cannot care for itself—wherever in America that family may live.
>
> Thus, for the first time, the government would recognize that it has no less of an obligation to the working poor than to the nonworking poor; and for the first time, benefits would be scaled in such a way that it would always pay to work.

But the thrust of the program was not exactly a new idea: "In the final analysis, we cannot talk our way out of poverty; we cannot legislate our way out of poverty; but this Nation can work its way out of poverty. What America needs now is not more welfare but more 'workfare.' "

The pushing and hauling within the administration continued. Moynihan viewed the proposals as the major domestic program which could help do politically for Nixon what Social Security had helped do for Franklin Roosevelt, namely, create a new political base. The working poor, already showing signs of their political alienation from liberal Democrats by their warm response to Gov. George Wallace, were available. But many Republicans did not seem to understand "political purchase through government benefits" **and** others argued that a tougher approach could do the same job—**cheaper**.

Meanwhile, it was Wilbur Mills's bill now. And he moved it along in his inimitable fashion. More sophisticated at the politics of welfare than Nixon (and pursuing his own interests), he quickly raised benefits for old persons, shifted much of the financial saving to the states from the South to the eastern and western industrial states (some observers attributed this to political motives relating to Mills preparing for a possible try for the speakership—or the presidency!) and added a number of effective, experience-based forced-work provisions designed to close the loopholes exposed through experience with WIN program and also to get decisions about work away from fuzzy-minded social workers and into the hands of tougher employment service bureaucrats. Mills steered the bill smoothly through the rocky shoals of conservative and liberal attack and sent H.R. 16311, The Family Assistance Act of 1970, to Russell Long in mid-April of 1970.

And there it died in the Finance Committee. Why? Some charged the President with nonsupport. Some felt both Nixon and Mills had gotten sufficient mileage out of FAP and preferred to let it lie until after the congressional elections of 1970. Long said it was because the bill did not have enough reform in it: "H.R. 16311 merely proposes to double the number of people on the rolls and more than double the cost. It would be more appropriately entitled 'The Welfare Expansion and Mess Perpetuation Bill' than a reform measure."

He particularly asserted that it not only lacked adequate work requirements but contained "fantastic, illogical incentives for people to quit work."

Before briefly looking at welfare reform **1971** style, let us remind ourselves that all this is **recent** history. It is accessible to you. You have been through it yourself. **You are there!** So you can decide why national welfare reform was postponed in 1970.

THE NIXON-MILLS WELFARE REFORM PLAN
COMES BACK—H.R. 1
In 1971, President Nixon sent welfare reform back to Congress.

I again urge the Congress to act in this session on welfare reform—so that going on welfare will not be more profitable
than going to work—so that we can bring under control a system that has become a suffocating burden on State and Local
taxpayers, and a massive outrage against the people it was
designed to help. . . .

Hard work is what made America great. There could be
no more dangerous delusion then the notion that we can
maintain the standard of living that our own people sometimes complain about but the rest of the world envies, without continuing to work hard. The "good life" is not the lazy
life, or the empty life or the life that consumes without pro-
ducing. The good life is the active, productive, working life—
the life that gives as well as gets. . . .

Let us recognize once and for all that any work is preferable
to welfare.

Wilbur Mills accepted it, assigned it highest priority, and
numbered it H.R. 1. He then set about improving it and gather-
ing the votes for passage. He put in some more money for old
people (an old **couple** is now to receive the same as a family
of four!) tightened up the forced work elements, saved the states
more money, and made a few other minor "improvements." Just
before reporting the bill out Mills showed he was a little edgy by
including the 10 percent Social Security increase he had been
keeping in his back pocket just for that purpose. (Sen. Robert
C. Byrd [Dem.-W. Va.] had commented in February, "It seems
to me it is an outrage to hold those poor old social security recipients as hostages, to hold their meager 10% increase hos-
tage to push through some kind of a legislative monstrosity.")

So Mills rode H.R. 1 through the rapids of liberal and conservative attack again. H.R. 1 passed the House on June 22,
1971.

WHAT IS IN THE 1971 NIXON-MILLS BILL H.R. 1?

It is beyond the scope of this book to present a detailed analysis of this complicated bill. You should get a copy of the bill, the House Ways and Means Committee report discussing it, similar material from the Senate Finance Committee and analyze the bill (or law, if it has passed!) for **yourself**!

The outlines of H.R. 1 as passed by the House are clear:

1. AFDC would be repealed.
2. In its place there would be **two** new programs.
   A. FAP—the Family Assistance Program for all families **without** an employable adult
   B. OFF—Opportunity for Families (they may not **call** it OFF) for families **with** an employable adult
3. The working poor would receive supplementary payments to a maximum combined work/"welfare" income of $4,320 for a family of four.
4. Every employable family member would be required to register for work and accept training except if ill, incapacitated, child under 16, or mother with preschool child (under 3 in 1973!).
5. "Adult" categories—old people, blind and disabled— would be federalized, placed under the Social Security Administration and receive phased-in benefits reaching $1,800 a year for a single person and $2,400 for a couple by 1973–74.
6. Welfare recipients would no longer be eligible for food stamps.
7. States would be "held harmless"—that is, not have to pay more as their share of the new family welfare program than they did as their share of the existing one (AFDC) in 1971.
8. Permits (but does **not** in any way require) states to supplement the federal benefit levels.

Those who favor the Nixon-Mills brand of welfare reform contend:

1. It establishes the principle of a guaranteed income floor.
2. It is a step in the right direction and can be improved later.
3. It will provide more money for the desperately poor in the South and for old people.
4. It will aid the working poor.
5. It will be federally administered, which will mean more equitable, less punitive administration.

Critics on the left argue:

1. The $2,400 floor is inadequate and will become a ceiling.
2. By calling it a step in the right direction it confuses people, hides what is really intended, and makes "real reform" harder to get.
3. 90% of all families on welfare now—all those in 45 states—will either get the same or **less** than they do now.
4. It has very bad forced-work provisions coupled with inadequate job-training and day-care opportunities.
5. Guarantees of due process and equal rights are omitted and legal gains of the last five years rolled back.
(For welfare recipients' critique of the bill and the administration's response, see pp. 158–72.)

Critics on the right say:

1. It establishes the guaranteed income principle!
2. It will result in a lobby of the poor pressing for higher and higher benefits.
3. It will double the welfare rolls and cost billions of dollars more than our present welfare system.
4. It takes away local and state rights to decide who gets welfare, to administer welfare their own way, and to decide how much welfare people "need" in their community.

NIXON-MILLS MEETS RIBICOFF-TALMADGE-LONG: H.R. 1 IN THE SENATE

As of this writing (early September 1972), H.R. 1 remains in the Senate Finance Committee. After more than a year, after hearings and committee work, Finance Committee Chairman Russell Long promised to report out a bill in mid-July 1972, but that has not happened. Most observers believe welfare reform is dead again for this session of Congress. If this is the case, the reasons are probably similar to those which caused the same result just prior to the 1970 election campaign. Conservative and progressive forces continue to oppose the FAP/H.R. 1 approach for opposite reasons. And President Nixon, in June 1972, rejected a compromise worked on by HEW Secretary Richardson, which was designed to bring together a bipartisan liberal coalition by Senator Ribicoff (Dem.-Conn.) to support a slightly liberalized version of the Nixon-Mills proposals.

Meanwhile several other things had happened which also undercut the forces pushing for welfare reform:

In December 1971, the Senate attached a package of amendments of the Work Incentive Program (WIN) to a tax bill. Authored by Sen. Herman Talmadge (Dem.-Ga.), these were aimed at "tightening up" work requirements for AFDC recipients. They were described by some as the "stick" provisions of H.R. 1 without its "carrots."

And on the other hand, Congress in late June 1972 took the increase in Social Security benefits out of the H.R. 1 package and passed it (in typical election-year fashion!).

These two actions served to take steam out of the push for welfare reform.

There were also several other important developments. A coalition of large industrial states and big-city forces formed, with Senator Ribicoff and Sen. Charles Percy (Rep.-Ill.) taking the lead. This coalition pressed for immediate fiscal relief for the states to be added into H.R. 1. They appeared, in November 1971, to reach agreement with the Administration on a plan to give the states approximately **$1 billion** in fiscal 1972, but this did **not** come to pass.

Then there was another struggle—this one with little public attention—in which the Administration sought to close off an existing provision which had been increasingly used by these same hard-pressed large state and city forces to get large amounts of federal money to pay for a variety of state services related to welfare. Again several **billions** of dollars were involved, and again some behind-the-scenes accommodation may have been reached.

Both these cases illustrate the pressures, magnitude, and forces involved around the fiscal aspects of welfare reform. These forces are still in motion. Perhaps additional fiscal relief for the states (and through them, big cities) will get added into the Nixon-Mills revenue-sharing proposals. Perhaps these forces may override other considerations to force further deliberation of welfare reform before this session of Congress adjourns.

Meanwhile, Russell Long has come up with his own welfare reform plan. In the spring of 1972 he announced that his plan had been passed by the Senate Finance Committee as a substitute for the Nixon-Mills Family Assistance Plan (Title 4) provisions of H.R. 1. The details of the Long plan have not been reported but the plan apparently centers around "guaranteed (and **required**) private and public employment." When announced, it was immediately attacked by Secretary of Labor James D. Hodgson as "an administrative nightmare" and a move toward "convict-type labor."

(As this was written, in October 1972, the Senate had just passed its version of H.R. 1. Both the Nixon-Mills/FAP and Long's plan were rejected and instead a major test of these and other plans was proposed. Many other complicated amendments to the present welfare system were included, together with numerous social security provisions. It was not clear whether the Senate and House versions of H.R. 1 could be reconciled in conference in time for a compromise version to be acted upon before Congress adjourned for the elections.)

So that's how it was (or at least seemed) when I wrote this! How is it with welfare reform as you are reading this? One way to keep things in focus is to develop your own ideas about alternatives. It is in that direction that we turn in the next chapter.

☞ DO-ITS

1. In 1961 the city manager of Newburgh, New York, using all the usual welfare reform themes, caught the public eye and established Newburgh as the symbol of get-tough on welfare. You can see exactly what happened in the CBS documentary The Battle of Newburgh available in most educational film libraries. Or read about it in Edgar May, The Wasted Americans (New York: Harper & Row, 1964).

2. When was the last wave of welfare reform in your city/state? Look at newspaper articles, reports, etc. and analyze what happened. Why was there a call for reform? What were the themes? What actually has it accomplished?

3. Visit whatever day-care and job-training programs that are operating in your area for welfare recipients. Talk with recipients and with staff people to find out the strengths and weaknesses of these programs.

4. Write your U. S. Congressman and/or U. S. Senators for copies of H.R. 1 as passed by the House and the House Ways and Means Committee Report on H.R. 1. Also ask for any available Senate (Finance Committee) materials.

5. Develop your own position on welfare reform. Are you for or against H.R. 1 as passed by the House? Why?

6. Talk to local and state welfare and employment service officials about how they think the Nixon-Mills FAP/OFF (or whatever is the current welfare reform proposal) would work in your area.

THE GAPS IN FAP

(The National Welfare Rights Organization's analysis of the Ways and Means Welfare Bill H.R. 1, "The Gaps in FAP" [May 24, 1971], prompted the U. S. Department of Health, Education, and Welfare to issue the NWRO material, adding its own rebuttal—"Administration Response to NWRO Grievances with Respect to H.R. 1" [July 1971]. Excerpts, giving both sides, are reprinted here. The HEW responses are in boldface type.)

1. *Payment level inadequate.* FAP sets a minimum and maximum payment of $2400 a year for a family of four. Payments would never go above $2400; there is no commitment to adequate income or to maintaining present payment levels in the 45 States where payments are now above $2400. The payment level is $1600 below the official poverty level and $4100 below $6500, the minimum amount a family needs to subsist at a decent level which is NWRO's position based on Department of Labor Surveys. NWRO's $6500 has been introduced by 21 members of Congress including the entire Black Caucus, H.R. 7257.

Response:

a. *Coverage of new groups and increased Federal benefits for the poorest current recipients*

It is not difficult to argue that $2400 is inadequate income for a family of four in most areas of the country. It is impossible, however, to argue that this level does not offer significant improvement in the life style and life chances of the 5 million children in working poor families plus those children living in the 22 States where the $2400 exceeds the current State payment level. This is especially true for persons in male-headed, working poor families. This group constitutes the major portion of new recipients, and is a group traditionally *not* represented by any organized group. The exclusion of this group from Federally-financed benefits has been a long-standing inequity which has seemed to be injurious to stable family life.

Given the need for fiscal responsibility, a hard choice has to be made for this welfare reform between substantially increasing benefits to those already covered—including recipients in the highest benefit level States—or broadening coverage and raising benefits for the poorest of the current recipients. Certainly the former strategy would be the more politically expedient course, for it would meet some of the demands of the organized recipient groups which draw their primary strength from high payment level cities and States. But this in itself would constitute no reform, and would only aggravate existing inequities between those covered and those not covered, and between those in poorer and those in more affluent States. Thus, we have opted for genuine structural reform which is far from punitive, especially with respect to the poorest of the poor and those heretofore excluded from assistance coverage. It is these latter groups who stand to gain or lose the most from the fate of H.R. 1.

Over 30 percent of the Nation's AFDC recipients are in the 22 States whose present payment is exceeded by $2400. In Mississippi, for example, families who must currently exist on $60 a month if they have no other income would receive $200 a month under H.R. 1. The $2400 Federal amount for a family of four, in combination with the $720 disregard for work-related expenses and the one-third disregard for earned income, assures that benefits will be paid to a family of four earning up to $4140, which is above the poverty level. A total of $2.3 billion[1] in additional income to low income children and adults would be provided under H.R. 1 during the first full year of program operation. It seems unlikely that these persons would argue that H.R. 1 is not a genuine improvement.

b. *States have strong financial inducements to raise benefits*
Not only is the basic Federal payment higher than the 30 percent the Nation's AFDC recipients are currently receiving, but most States are expected to *raise* their benefits by an amount equal to the applicable food stamp bonus for families at the current State payment level. The fiscal protection provision allows States to raise their supplement by this amount and qualify for total protection based on 1971 calendar costs *even if they do not now participate in the food stamp program.* Thus it is likely that as many as 75 percent of current recipients will be better off under H.R. 1 than they are now.

---

[1] And this figure includes only 6 months of payments to families in which both parents are present, neither is incapacitated, and the father is employed (i.e., the "working poor"). The effective date for this provision is January 1, 1973.

c. *Many recipients have some income*

Too often the basic Federal floor is conceived of as the level at which most recipient families must live. In fact, relatively few families have no income at all—whether earned by adults or children, or "unearned." Over two-thirds of all potentially eligible family heads will have some income from employment, and many families will receive child support payments and the benefits of other public programs. Such families will obviously have incomes considerably higher than $2400 after the application of the income disregards and income supplementation features of H.R. 1.

Additionally, however, are the many persons with no current income who will be drawn into the labor market through the provision of more than 875,000 child care slots, the 700,000 slots for manpower training and placement activities, 75,000 slots for job upgrading, and the estimated 200,000 public service jobs to be created under H.R. 1. Moreover, exclusive focus on $2400 ignores the role of State supplementation, particularly with respect to adjustments this provides for cost of living differences.

d. *Trade-off between benefit level, incentives, and break-even level*

In any well-structured program with built-in work incentives, benefit levels cannot be considered in isolation from costs and caseloads. Given a particular incentive rate (or proportion of earnings which reduces benefits), the basic payment level will determine the break-even point at which families receive no further supplementation. As the Committee Report notes: "Increasing it (the basic benefit level) by $100 . . . , and keeping other parts of the benefit structure the same, raises the break-even point by $150, increases the cost by over $500 million per year and the number of eligible families by 300 thousand. The cost of such increases in general gets progressively higher: i.e., each additional $100 in the basic benefit costs more than the preceding one. The reason for this effect is quite simple—there are more families with earnings in each higher $100 interval. This effect would continue until the level of the break-even point exceeds average family earnings for the whole Nation." [2]

The $2400 minimum represents a reasonable compromise between costs and adequacy of level, especially in view of its institution as a new Federal program. NWRO's proposal for a $6500 minimum for a family of four would cost $70 billion over the present system and cover more than one-half of the U.S. population.

e. *No disruption of regional economies*

The purposes of a program of this sort—to provide basic income support and supplementation of family income—would be totally defeated if the impact on local economies was widespread disruption, closing of industries, and loss of jobs. Arguments to the effect that depressed localities must suffer the consequences ignore the fact that the primary burden would be borne by those least able to help themselves and those with few other opportunities. Rather than ignore the potential for such disruption, benefit levels must be geared to mesh with and promote economic development. In our view, the basic level of $2400 can offer vital and healthy stimulation to local economies and avoid undesirable effects.

Here again, it is important to consider the division of labor between National and State programs, and not expect either to fulfill the functions of both. The Federal Government's role is to provide a floor; that of the States to adjust benefits upward if necessary to correspond to area costs of living and wage levels.

• • •

3. *Nine out of ten welfare families could be worse off.* $2400 a year, $200 a month is above present payment levels for only 10 percent of the welfare families, those in Alabama, Arkansas,

[2] Page 219, House Report No. 92-231.

Louisiana, Mississippi and South Carolina. In addition, poor families in Puerto Rico, the Virgin Islands and Guam will receive less than $2400—$1330 in Puerto Rico even though the cost-of-living on that island is 20 percent higher than in Washington, D.C. Recipients in the Virgin Islands and Guam along with those in the other 45 States, 90 percent of the families, could receive less than the meager payments they receive under the current welfare system. While payments go up in five southern States and Puerto Rico, Mississippi and Puerto Rico will be the only places where the increases will be substantial.

Response:

Over thirty percent of the Nation's AFDC recipients are in the 22 States whose present *payment* level (as contrasted to need standard) is exceeded by the $2400. Four States in addition to those mentioned have payment levels below $2400 and no food stamp program anywhere in the State. Many others make food stamps available only in a few counties (7 of 71 in Florida, for example). We estimate that some 25% of the Nation's AFDC recipients will have benefit increases due to the $2400 base alone.

How can NWRO ignore the poor families in Mississippi receiving $60/month for four by opposing a bill which *raises their benefits to $200/month?* How does NWRO explain its opposition to H.R. 1 to the working poor families with five million children who now receive no payment but would get substantial coverage (benefits up to a cut-off earnings level of $4140 for a four person family)?

Under current law, families not only "could be worse off" they *are* being made worse off. At least ten States have reduced or soon will reduce payments (New York, of course, already has). This bill provides the fiscal protection to States to *allow them to maintain levels,* and in fact increase levels.

• • •

4. *States would be encouraged to reduce payments.* State governments will not have to spend more than they spend during

calendar year 1971 no matter how many more people get on welfare. The Federal Government will pay for the costs due to more people getting on welfare. However, if States increase payments above the amount recipients received in cash and food stamps combined as of January 1, 1971, the States will have to pay the entire cost of these increases. While the $2400 payment means most States will save money in the first years of the plan, they are not likely to pass this money along to poor people. Most States will keep the savings because they now spend more than they want to on welfare.

In fact, States may cut the amount they spend on welfare. No State is required to maintain present payment levels. They can cut back to the Federal $2400 and not spend anything on welfare. By reducing payments, States can save even more than they would by maintaining benefits. It will be much easier for States to cut benefits under FAP than under the present system which requires that a State percentage reduction plan be approved by HEW.

Response:
There is absolutely no encouragement to a State to reduce payment levels; on the contrary, there are strong incentives built into the hold-harmless provision for benefit *increases*. States can provide the full cash value of food stamps (at Federal expense) even if they do not now participate in the food stamp program. It will not be easier to cut benefits than under current law (States are completely free to set their own payment level, and at least fourteen States have reduced or soon will reduce payments).

To say a State may cut back to $2400 can only be compared to saying that under current law they can cut back to $0. Baseless speculation about our State and local government's lack of responsibility to its citizens serves no constructive purpose, and only confuses the basic point: a $2400 *floor* is being set for the first time in all States.

In many States the Federal benefit levels will be such that the State itself will have virtually a 100 percent saving in

current welfare costs and the costs of administration. Such States would, we believe, have strong incentives to use some of this money to provide State supplements to the Federal benefit level.

• • •

7. *Discrimination against single individuals, childless couples, families and against Blacks.* FAP provides benefits only for families with children. Single individuals and couples without children receive no benefits whatsoever, unless they are aged, disabled or blind. They must rely on almost nonexistent State and local relief programs.

Families with children would receive only half as much as the aged, disabled and blind. While a family of four receives $200 a month, by July, 1973 an aged couple will receive the same amount.

Half of the families on welfare are Black. Only 1/5 of the aged, disabled and blind recipients are Black. The program that is largely Black will pay half as much as the program that is largely white.

Response:
The bill does not cover approximately 1 million single individuals and childless couples living in poverty who are not aged, blind, or disabled. H.R. 1 concentrates funds available for family benefits upon poor children, a difficult decision but arguable in that children may provide the best means of breaking the dependency cycle. Some States, localities and other organizations do provide General Assistance or emergency relief to single persons or childless couples and presumably they will continue to do so.

The argument that H.R. 1 discriminates against Black families when compared to the largely white adult categories is extremely misleading. First it must be noted that the adult categories have historically received higher benefits than families on the presumption that the employment potential of the aged, blind and disabled is extremely limited while their special needs may be greater.

Next, it stretches credibility to claim that a program which pays benefits to aged, blind, or disabled people, without regard to race, is a racist program.

H.R. 1 is designed to help poor people—without regard to race.

• • •

8. *The forced work requirement is more repressive and punitive than the present law.* In the light of growing unemployment these provisions will only serve to deny benefits to needy people, harass innocent citizens, destroy family life and deny real opportunities for advancement. Families with members considered employable will be referred to OFF, "Opportunities for Families," a separate program run by the Labor Department. Recipients who refuse to participate will be thrown off welfare. However, the lack of adequate training, child care and employment provisions means no real opportunities, only harassment for poor people.

Response:
We believe adults in welfare families who are able to work want to work. Indeed, a consistent goal of NWRO has been greater employment opportunities for welfare recipients. H.R. 1 substantially steps up Federal efforts to provide training, employment guidance, child care, and public service jobs. It is difficult to construe these efforts as "harassment" rather than "real opportunities." It is not true that work "destroys family life"; on the contrary, it is well established that work fosters independence and pride—on the part of the children as well as the adults.

Most responsible organizations of welfare recipients believe that a good job and an end to welfare payments should be the goals of all employable recipients.

• • •

9. *Mothers with children over 3 years old will be forced to work.* All family members will be required to register and accept a job offer unless they are specifically exempted. Under present law only those specifically referred to work are forced to register. Mothers of children over three and children over sixteen and not in school are among those not exempted and forced to work. Mothers with a father in the home who registers need not register. But if there is no father in the home the mother will be forced out of the home into a job.

Response:
First, the administration opposed the move to require mothers to register who have children under six (and in fact, during the first two years of the program the limit is age six). We believe that there are situations in which the interests of the children are best served by personal care by the mother until children reach school age. An additional factor of course, is the present scarcity of good child care, especially for children ages three to five.

There is, however, a real equity problem involved. Over seven out of ten non-welfare mothers who are widowed, divorced, or otherwise without a man in the house, *do work.* It seems unreasonable to expect less of one group than economic necessity imposes on another.

Also, it is entirely consistent with national trends to expect mothers of school-age children to work. More than half of all mothers with children age six to seventeen are in the labor force, compared with one-third in 1950. Indeed, women—including welfare recipients—are making increasingly vocal demands for child care and other arrangements to permit them to so participate.

• • •

19. *Jobs for welfare recipients are not available.* a) The punitive nature of the forced work requirement assumes that jobs are available for welfare mothers and b) that the rolls are filled

with employable people who simply refuse to work. Neither assumption is correct. The 1969 HEW study of Aid to Families with Dependent Children reports that 20.1% of welfare mothers are in the labor market. Of these, 66.5% are working. 33.5% are unemployed—looking for work but unable to find it. This is over five times the national unemployment rate.

c) Governor Reagan of California wrote to 309,485 employers in the State asking each to hire one welfare recipient. Only 13,000 employers responded. A total of 337 jobs were reported but only 26 actual jobs resulted from the effort. The average salary was $71.00 a week.

Response:
a) **The penalties in the law would not operate if a welfare recipient had no job to go to. The bill provides $800 million during the first year for public service jobs and 225,000 new training slots. The bill includes many other incentives to provide work for welfare recipients.**
b) **The work requirement does not imply that the welfare rolls are filled with employable people who refuse to work. The bill is, however, constructed around the assumption that many recipients both can work and want to work. A recent study by HEW supports this assumption. The study found that the proportion of AFDC women with high employment potential increased from 25.3 percent in 1961 to 44.5 percent in 1968. Thus, it is reasonable to expect that almost half of the AFDC mothers can be moved into regular employment, with training, child care, and concentrated employment efforts. The report stated that "as the AFDC caseload grew ever larger between 1961 and 1968, recipients were more and more women who had stronger educational and occupational backgrounds, that is, high employment potential." However, the report also notes that over 80 percent of the women reportedly could not take jobs because they had children under age eight at home, and more than 50**

percent lacked child care facilities. To compensate for the current lack of child care and to enable mothers to take advantage of employment and training opportunities, the bill provides for 875,000 day care slots and permits deductions for the cost of child care directly purchased.

c) The implication of the NWRO statement is that a job with a salary of $71 a week is not worth having. In fact, with Federal supplementation alone the total income for a family of four would be $4,112—exclusive of day care subsidy or State supplementation. Assuming 50 weeks of work at 40 hours a week, the hourly wage including supplementation is $2.05.

• • •

20. *Legal and Constitutional Rights.* Recipients would have fewer legal rights under FAP than they have now. The few legal rights to welfare poor people enjoy under current law are seriously undermined or outright denied by H.R. 1. Several provisions fly in the face of constitutionally protected rights to equal protection and due process of law. Many provisions further demean poor people and destroy their family life, dignity and pride and make them less able to stand on their own.

Response:
The provisions in H.R. 1 relating to the legal rights of recipients are designed specifically to afford every opportunity for equal protection and due process. An individual is given 30 days in which to request a hearing regarding determinations of eligibility and benefit amount with which he disagrees. A decision would be rendered within 90 days. The Secretary's decision would be subject to judicial review in Federal district courts except in determinations as to fact. Furthermore, qualified persons not meeting requirements of the Administrative Procedures Act would be permitted to act as hearings examiners. This would allow a much broader

source of examiners. Under the bill, no attorneys' fees would be withheld from a person's benefits. Hearings would be conducted in accordance with the Administrative Procedures Act and the protective rules on the representation of claimants under the social security program would apply.

Other provisions requiring work or training are designed to help poor people to become self-sufficient and regain a sense of dignity and pride in themselves. Provisions allowing the eligibility of the working poor and families headed by unemployed males are intended to strengthen family bonds and discourage family break-up in order to receive welfare.

• • •

25. *There is no limit on parents' support obligations.* Even if a mother or father cannot afford to support the children, a parent who leaves home would be obligated to the United States Government for every cent the family receives from FAP unless the amount of support payments were fixed by a court order. If no court order has been issued, the ability of the parent to pay is not permitted to be a factor in limiting his or her liability. Many fathers do in fact leave their wives and children because they cannot afford to support them. Parents who travel in inter-state commerce to avoid supporting their children are subject to a fine of $1,000, a year in prison, or both.

Response:
H.R. 1 marks a significant departure from traditional welfare policy in its extension of assistance to intact, male-headed families where the father is employed. The bill thus reflects the recognition that low income from employment, or the loss of full-time employment may place severe strains on families. This provision should eliminate the alleged need for a father to desert in order for his family to qualify for welfare, and it is appropriate that he be required to support his family. Writing on this subject, D. P. Moynihan stated: ". . . the poor of

the United States today enjoy a quite unprecedented freedom to abandon their children in the certain knowledge that society will care for them, and what is more, in a State such as New York, to care for them by quite decent standards. . . . Now, a working-class or middle-class American who chooses to leave his family is normally required first to go through elaborate legal proceedings and thereafter to devote much of his income to supporting them. Normally speaking, society gives him nothing. The fathers of AFDC families, however, simply disappear. Only a person invincibly prejudiced on behalf of the poor would deny that there are attractions in such freedom of movement."

Recipient organizations and other observers of public policy have for some time deplored the corrosive effects of current welfare policy on family stability, and have argued that welfare policy should at least be neutral but at best encourage family stability. The cash benefits to male-headed families under H.R. 1 will effectively work toward this end, and the provision enforcing parental obligations will provide whatever additional strength that may be required.

In order to discourage abandonment of families, H.R. 1 provides that a deserting parent would owe the U.S. the amount of assistance benefits paid to the spouse and children during the period of desertion, reduced by any amount he paid to his family during that period. The penalty for interstate flight to avoid parental support responsibilities does not seem too severe in view of the fact that desertion is a major cause of the expanding AFDC caseload and thus the cost of supporting the families is rapidly increasing. Because it is more likely that an intact family would be able to work itself off the welfare rolls than one in which a parent has deserted, it is important that parental obligations be enforced, and there is a long-standing body of law and social attitude in support of this requirement.

• • •

31. *Advisory committees may exclude recipients.* Advisory committees to evaluate the program would be composed of representatives of labor, business, the public and the government. Representatives of recipients and recipient organizations are not specified.

Response:
H.R. 1 provides for the establishment of local advisory committees to study and evaluate the effectiveness of the program. They are to be composed of representatives of labor, business, units of local government, and the public. Recipients, of course, are in the latter category, and since evaluation of the program clearly requires information and advice from recipients, we can expect recipients to be on most if not all of such committees.

Are HEW's Responses Convincing to You?

Check with your local WRO or Social Workers' Union for rebuttal! Two other important sources for analysis and comment on welfare legislation are:

1. Center on Social Welfare Policy and Law
   401 West 117th Street, New York, N.Y. 10027
2. Elizabeth Wickenden
   c/o National Assembly for Social Policy and Development, Inc.
   345 East 46th Street, New York, N.Y. 10017

☞ CHAPTER SEVEN
ALTERNATIVES TO WELFARE

Although a detailed discussion of the proliferating "income maintenance" alternatives is not possible in this book, it probably doesn't matter too much anyway. Although many "welfare reform" and guaranteed-income plans have been proposed and discussed over the last five years, most of the interest has been shown by the technicians, not the public.

It will take a considerable change in both political reality and the way in which we use welfare economically, for any of these more human schemes of "welfare reform" to become viable as replacements for the welfare system. But we will run through them once lightly trying to suggest resources for further study if you are so inclined.

CONGRESSIONAL ALTERNATIVES TO THE NIXON-MILLS PLAN

Three major alternatives to the Nixon-Mills plan were proposed in the 92d Congress (1971–72):

1. The National Welfare Rights Organization (NWRO) Adequate Income Plan was introduced in the House by the Black Caucus and cosponsored by twenty-one Congressmen (H.R. 7257). Sen. George McGovern (Dem.-S. Dak.) introduced the same measure in the Senate (S 2372). (See pp. 181–95 for NWRO's explanation of this proposal.) It would set welfare benefits at $6,500 per year for a family of four (based on BLS

lower income level updated to rise in cost of living **and** national median income). NWRO has used their adequate income alternative as a model "welfare reform" act to educate, rally support, etc.

2. A second measure designed principally as an educational effort is the proposal developed initially by the loose liberal coalition called the Campaign for Adequate Welfare Reform Now. National church groups, League of Women Voters, and social welfare groups like the National Association of Social Workers developed this alternative to embody minimum due-process guarantees and progress toward an adequate income goal through starting at the poverty line and increasing within several years to the BLS lower living level. This measure was introduced in the House as H.R. 7388 by Congressman Donald Frazier (Dem.-Minn.) and in the Senate as S 2747 by Sen. Fred Harris (Dem.-Okla.).

3. Sen. Abraham Ribicoff (Dem.-Conn.) introduced a package of amendments to H.R. 1 (Amendment No. 559) designed to soften its harshest forced-work features, restore some due-process protections, slightly raise benefits (to $3,000 a year for a family of four), and at the same time provide maximum fiscal relief to the states. The Ribicoff amendments became the focal point for a liberal-led effort to ensure that some kind of welfare reform with attendant benefits to the large industrial states passed the 92d Congress.

PAST PROPOSALS OF NOTE
In the debates over welfare reform of the last five years, three national studies have played a part.

The first grew out of the Newburgh reform wave and took the form of an Advisory Council on Public Welfare created under the 1962 Social Security amendments. Its report, issued in June 1966, "Having the Power, We Have the Duty" (from a quotation of President Johnson), recommended "that adequate financial aid and social services be available to all who need them as a matter of right." To implement this, the council proposed that the federal government set nationwide standards

ALTERNATIVES TO WELFARE

and greatly increase federal financing. In greatly watered down form, the council's report formed the basis for President Johnson's proposals which served as a point of departure for Mills's 1967 program. One important survival was a provision requiring cost-of-living increases in AFDC which after a vigorous NWRO-led fight and much litigation led to grant increases in about half the states by 1970. Other items from the report that were included in the 1967 Social Security amendments or in HEW regulations were more services, greater protection of legal rights, and increased use of volunteers and nonprofessionals.

As a guaranteed-income proposal this wasn't very much of one—essentially of the "improve welfare" variety.

The second report of national significance came from a group of businessmen convened by Gov. Nelson Rockefeller, at least in part as a domestic issue attention-getter, as he was seeking the Republican Presidential nomination for 1968. Headed by Joseph C. Wilson, chairman of the board of Xerox, this committee produced in November 1967 the "Arden House Report" (named after the place of the meeting). Their recommendation was to replace public assistance with "an income maintenance system, possibly a negative income tax, which would bring all 30 million poor Americans up to at least the official Federal poverty line."

They also were for family planning, more research especially of "systems" variety, and were worried that "the nation stands in danger of being torn apart." Despite the high-level corporate executives who comprised it, the committee did not have much impact. Either their hearts weren't in it or Rockefeller lost interest when he didn't get nominated.

Meanwhile, President Johnson, a few months before his decision not to seek reelection, had employed a creative variant of the crisis-outcry/study/reform sequence—the crisis-outcry/reform/**then** study plan. He created and appointed a commission on income maintenance (President's Commission on Income Maintenance) as he signed the Mills-Long 1967 amendments in January 1968, partly to keep his options open by cooling the liberal—especially labor—opposition. Also he (like we) may have been curious to see if there **really** was a better idea than welfare.

In November 1969 the PCIM reported to the new President. Nixon had already announced his welfare reform as the cornerstone of his domestic policy and so was unlikely to be very much influenced by the study. The PCIM report is excellent. With the possible exception noted by commission member Julian Samora that "we looked at a number of plans but most were old and conventional, including the one that was chosen by the majority," the study was thoroughgoing. The result predictably was less than revolutionary. The main recommendation was for "creation of a universal income supplement program financed and administered by the federal government making cash payments to all of the population with income needs." The PCIM suggested a starting level of $2,400 for a family of four not because "it is an adequate income but because it is a practical program that can be implemented in the near future." Obviously the commission was concerned about having to deal with a new President who had already set his own program. They chose to stay close to the Nixon proposals and try to move them a little. Since Nixon-Mills #2 accepts their level ($2,400) one might think that strategy worked. My own estimate is that despite a small lobbying effort by the commission, some public relations, a model bill, etc. the report was "filed and forgotten" like so many past studies. It might have been a little different if Ben Heineman, commission chairman, was a Nixon friend and appointee instead of a Johnson-Humphrey man or if he had taken his own advice about political hard work making a higher income floor more politically possible given only a few months earlier before a Senate committee.

Now let us look at the range of guaranteed annual-income proposals.

THE GUARANTEED INCOME
The **idea** apparently was "invented" (or at least popularized) in modern times by Robert Theobald. He is one of the few, however, who seem primarily concerned with using it as "an al-

ternative future" as compared with many who seek either to preserve the status quo or at best tinker a little with it.*

THE NEGATIVE INCOME TAX
Part of the appeal of this plan probably arises from our identification with the idea of income tax as **negative**! Once explained it is simple enough—either you have income and pay **positive** income tax or you have none (or less than a certain amount) and the government pays you. Milton Friedman, economist and adviser to Barry Goldwater, started this idea in 1962. Since then, there have been a wide range of negative income tax plans ranging from "big" ones like NWRO's to "little" ones like FAP. None are as "little" as Friedman's because he proposed to substitute a modest negative tax for a great many other government programs—as many as possible (like public housing, veterans benefits, unemployment compensation, farm subsidies, maybe even public schools!). James Tobin, former member of the President's economic advisory council, is another NIT enthusiast. Some of the literature:

1. James Tobin, Joseph A. Pechsman, and Peter M. Mieszkowski, "Is a Negative Income Tax Practical?" **Yale Law Journal,** Vol. 77, No. 1, Nov. 1967; also available as reprint 142 (Washington: The Brookings Institution, 1967).
2. Christopher Green, **Negative Taxes and the Poverty Problem** (Washington: The Brookings Institution).
3. George H. Hildebrand, **Poverty, Income Maintenance, and the Negative Income Tax** (Ithaca: New York State School of Industrial Relations, Cornell University, 1967).
4. Milton Friedman, **Capitalism and Freedom** (Chicago: University of Chicago Press, 1962), chaps. 6 and 10.

* See Robert Theobald, **The Guaranteed Income, Next Step in Socioeconomic Revolution** (Garden City, N.Y.: Doubleday Anchor Books, 1967) for background, philosophy, economics, and variations.

FAMILY OR CHILDREN'S ALLOWANCES

Daniel Patrick Moynihan, in the days before he went to work for President Nixon, advocated this kind of plan which would pay an allowance to **all** families regardless of need. Most other industrial nations have long since adopted some variation of the family allowance. Advantages include the fact that since the middle class also receives this "welfare," they will support it politically (and not leave the poor to fend for themselves). This also is a disadvantage though, since because many nonpoor people get the allowance it is very costly and, therefore, usually must be set so low that it doesn't lift many poor people out of poverty. Michigan economist Harvey Brazer has a very clever solution: Give it to everyone then tax it back from those who don't need it! (My own favorite, since I know I would be pleased to receive a government payment for my children, and not likely miss the increased taxes which recovered it!)

Another key issue is whether or not children's allowances encourage people to have more children.

Principal children's allowance advocates include Alvin L. Schorr, whose **Poor Kids: A Report on Children in Poverty** (New York: Basic Books, Inc., 1966) explores all the issues, and James C. Vadakin (**Children, Poverty, and Family Allowances** [New York: Basic Books, Inc., 1968]), who has studied this system extensively.

The influential Citizens Committee for Children of New York held a conference on children's allowances in 1967 as part of their effort to build support for such a plan. The conference report is another good source of family and children's allowance plan information including the Brazer plan referred to above (**Children's Allowances and the Economic Welfare of Children,** Citizens Committee for Children of New York, Inc., 112 E. 19th Street, New York 10003, 1968).

A plan where **everybody** (not just families with children) gets an allowance called a "social dividend" was proposed in England by Lady Rhys-Williams during World War II but has received little attention in this country. Sen. George McGovern (Dem.-S. Dak.) recently talked about this type of plan.

OTHER INCOME MAINTENANCE IDEAS

The foregoing are the main plans being talked about but here are a few others which can be briefly noted:

1. Government Guaranteed Work. See Garth L. Mangum, "Government as Employer of Last Resort," in Levitan, Cohen, and Lampman, eds., **Toward Freedom from Want** (Madison: Industrial Research Association, 1968).
2. The Second Income Plan. A plan to make income from **capital** (stock dividends) available to the poor. See Louis O. Kelso and Patricia Hetter, **Two Factor Theory: The Economics of Reality** (New York: Random House, 1968).
3. "Mothers' Wages." David Gil of Brandeis University has proposed that "society should pay an appropriate wage to every mother . . . for as long as childbearing and rearing tasks keep them outside the labor market."

And on the other hand, a New York woman argues that "the community should give to every woman of childbearing age whose income is at or below the poverty level . . . a $500 bonus every year that she does **NOT** have a baby."

Finally, it should be pointed out that many people simply favor combining these approaches with existing programs in some fashion. For example, Alvin Schorr says, "We must raise minimum benefit levels in social security more rapidly than those at the top and have a serious look at new social security programs that are needed—children's allowances and federal long term unemployment insurance in particular."

In testimony before the President's Commission on Income Maintenance, Beulah Sanders of New York, now chairman of NWRO, eloquently reminds us of another issue: "Let me begin by saying that whatever changes this Commission recommends in the welfare system . . . will have no meaning and will not begin to meet the problems of poverty in America unless welfare recipients gain control over the programs that serve them." **Her** plan is simple: "Everybody from President Nixon on down is talking about us. Everyone has their own plan on what to do with welfare recipients. Well, the only thing you can really do is get up off your 17th Century attitudes, give poor people enough money to live decently, and let us decide how to live our lives."

WHAT IS YOUR PLAN?

☞ DO-ITS

1. If you are interested in the religious and moral issues involved in the guaranteed income idea see Philip Wogaman, Guaranteed Annual Income, The Moral Issues **(Nashville: Abingdon Press, 1968).**
2. **The basic economic and social elements of** inequality **(a broader concept than** poverty) **are analyzed in S. M. Miller and Pamela Roby,** The Future of Inequality **(New York: Basic Books, Inc., 1970).**
3. **Surprisingly, little has been written about what the social consequences of adequate income for all might be. Two articles which begin to think about the almost unthinkable possibilities are: David Hapgood, "Beyond Welfare Reform,"** The Washington Monthly, **May 1970; and Margaret Mead, "Some Social Consequences of a Guaranteed Income," Robert Theobald, ed.,** Committed Spending, A Route to Economic Security **(Garden City, N.Y.: Doubleday Anchor Books, 1969).**

THE NWRO ADEQUATE INCOME PLAN

$6500 NOW!

NATIONAL WELFARE RIGHTS ORGANIZATION

2

As the rich get richer the poor get poorer.
In 1970 it took $5500 for a family of four to
support themselves adequately. In 1971 it takes $6500 . . . .

The National Welfare Rights Organization is a nationwide organization of welfare recipients and other low income Americans. We have over 800 local affiliates in all 50 states and in more than 400 cities. Our members - Blacks, whites, Indians, Chicanos, Puerto Ricans - have joined together in a struggle to change the system that oppresses us, to demand Adequate Income, Dignity, Justice and Democracy.

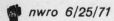 *nwro 6/25/71*

THE WELFARE CRISIS

NWRO says there is a welfare crisis in the United States today. Despite the growing number of people on welfare, over one fourth of the country's population cannot afford to provide themselves with the basic necessities of life: food, clothing and shelter. The country is not yet willing to find a solution to assure their welfare. NWRO says that solution exists and it is up to the government to make it a reality.

NWRO challenges the government to change its priorities from death and destruction to life and peace. We call upon the government to stop subsidizing the rich and the corporations who need it least and start assuring an adequate income for all Americans (through wages, welfare, or both). The richest 20% of the population today has 43% of the income while the poorest 20% has only 6%. We demand that the government move now to assure EVERYONE an adequate income.

3

$5500 TO $6500

In 1969 NWRO first devised an Adequate Income Plan. We calculated that a family of four needed $5500 to survive at a minimum but adequate level of health and decency. In 1971 it takes $6500. The change from $5500 to $6500 is not a change in our Plan. We are simply following our Plan by keeping grant levels consistent with the rise in U.S. living costs.

HOW THE ADEQUATE INCOME PLAN WORKS

ANYONE WITH AN INADEQUATE INCOME IS ELIGIBLE.

All Americans are assured a basic standard of income, $2250 for a single individual and $6500 for a family of four. Payments vary according to family size.

4

NWRO PLAN PAYMENT LEVELS FOR DIFFERENT SIZED FAMILIES

FAMILY SIZE	INCOME PER	YEAR	MONTH	WEEK
One person		$2250	$188	$43
Two people		4100	342	79
Three people		5300	442	102
Four people		6500	542	125
Five people		7700	642	148

$1200 a year for each additional family member

**THE INCOME LEVEL
CHANGES WITH CHANGES IN PRICES AND
WITH CHANGES IN THE AVERAGE FAMILY'S INCOME.**

To prevent those families receiving Adequate Income payments from becoming poorer as prices and the average family's income rise the payment level will be adjusted annually.

**THE INCOME LEVEL IS ADJUSTED FOR
DIFFERENT COSTS OF LIVING IN DIFFERENT PLACES.**

In rural areas and the smaller urban places, the amounts will be less than shown above. In large cities the amounts will be higher. The $6500 is an urban average budget. Figures for specific places are shown on the following page.

ALTERNATIVES TO WELFARE

NWRO PLAN PAYMENT LEVELS
FOR DIFFERENT PLACES

AREA ....AMOUNT PER YEAR

Urban United States $6500
Non-metropolitan areas $6110

Atlanta,Georgia $5980
Baltimore, Maryland $6565
Boston, Massachusetts $6890
Chicago, Illinois $6760
Cincinnati, Ohio $6175
Cleveland, Ohio $6630
Dallas, Texas $6240
Denver, Colorado $6240
Detroit, Michigan $6500
Hartford, Connecticut $7085
Honolulu, Hawaii $8060
Houston, Texas $6045
Indianapolis, Indiana $6630
Kansas City, Missouri $6500
Los Angeles, California $7020
Milwaukee, Wisconsin $6630
Minneapolis, Minnesota $6695
Nashville, Tennessee $5915
New York, New York $6695
Philadelphia, Pennsylvania $6500
Pittsburgh, Pennsylvania $6240
St. Louis, Missouri $6500
San Francisco, California $7150
Seattle, Washington $7150

5

EMERGENCY NEEDS ARE MET.

The Plan also provides grants for clothing and furniture and clothing to bring participant's households up to minimum standards of health and decency at the time they first come into the Plan. Replacement costs are provided in cases of flood, fire, or any other substantial change in the family's circumstance.

The Bureau of Labor Statistics assumed in computing the budget that the family had been established for fifteen years and had an accumulated stock of clothing and furniture. The budget was intended only to cover replacements. This assumption does not apply to the average family living in poverty. Emergency grants are necessary for furnishings and wardrobe to bring persons up to minimum standards of health and decency and to meet disasters if they occur.

PLAN PROVIDES FOR WORK INCENTIVE BUT NO FORCED WORK.

Most of the recipients are working people who do not earn adequate wages. The Adequate Income Plan provides a work incentive by allowing recipients to retain the entire cost of all purchases made in connection with the job such as child care, transportation, uniforms and tools and union dues plus one third of the earnings above this amount. An amount equal to the remaining two-thirds will be deducted from the Adequate Income payment. For example, if a man with a wife and two children earns $100 a week above his work-related expenses, two thirds of this amount is deducted from the Adequate Income payment of $125 for a family of four. They would be left with a payment of $125 - $67 = $58. This is $58 a week more than he would get without the Adequate Income Plan. No forced work requirement is necessary. Recipients will work if given a good opportunity.

6

THOSE NOT ELIGIBLE FOR PAYMENTS MAY PAY LOWER INCOME TAXES.

Under NWRO's Plan a family of four is eligible for benefits until its earned income reaches just under $12,000 a year. Families earning up to $9,750 receive actual payments as described above. Families earning over $9,750 can also benefit because

186

they pay income taxes at a reduced rate until their earnings reach $11,461. At this point a family of four would begin paying taxes at the normal rate. The chart below compares how the final income of a family of four is affected by NWRO's Plan and by the present (1973) Federal income tax law at various earning levels.

FINAL INCOME UNDER NWRO PLAN COMPARED WITH INCOME UNDER 1973 TAX LAW.

Earnings	NWRO Plan-Payment		Final Income Under NWRO Plan		Under 1973 Tax Law
$ 0	+	$6500	=	$6500	vs. $2248*
2000	+	5167	=	7167	vs. 2000
3000	+	4500	=	7500	vs. 3000
4000	+	3833	=	7833	vs. 4000
5000	+	3167	=	8167	vs. 4860
7500	+	1498	=	8998	vs. 6476
9000	+	500	=	9500	vs. 7589
9750	+	0	=	9750	vs. 8231
10000	−	167	=	9833	vs. 8445
11461	−	1114	=	10317	vs. 10317

*Average welfare payment under current law.

7

PEOPLE IN UNIQUE SITUATIONS COULD GET A LARGER BASIC PAYMENT.

Participants have the right to choose between the basic payment level of the Plan or an itemized budget of their own needs which would consider actual costs of housing, clothing, or any special problem not reflected in the basic budget. This is similar to the income tax system in which an individual can take the standard deduction or itemize his or her deductions, whichever gives great - er benefits.

The budget is based on statistical averaging form- ulas which do not necessarily apply to real people or real situations. For example, an individual family of four may or may not be able to obtain adequate housing in good condition at the $92 a month rent that the budget allows, even if that happens to be the average for the city in which he lives.

**BENEFITS WILL BE EASY TO OBTAIN
IF THE APPLICANT IS ELIGIBLE.**

There will be no harassment of applicants of the type which prevents recipients from receiving aid under the present welfare system. Eligibility is to be based solely on need under NWRO's Plan and is determined by a person's declaration of what his needs are, with spot checks, as is done under our income tax system. All rights and regulations under the Adequate Income Plan are written in simple and understandable language. The Plan is administered by a single agency, located in the Federal government, with standards and procedures uniform throughout the country.

8

**LEGAL AND CONSTITUTIONAL RIGHTS
OF RECIPIENTS WILL BE PROTECTED.**

Participants in the Plan are entitled to a fair hearing prior to the reduction or termination of benefits. The hearing must take place within 15 days of the application for appeal. Special grants are provided for legal fees, child care, and other expenses associated with appeals. Fair hearing decisions may be appealed in the courts.

**SOCIAL SERVICES AND MEDICAID
ARE AVAILABLE ON A VOLUNTARY BASIS.**

Services of all kinds, controlled by participants would include family and vocational counselling, homemaker services, family planning, child care, other educational programs, legal and medical services. While making no specific provisions our plan assumes that these services will be free and located in the recipient's community.

WHERE NWRO'S BUDGET COMES FROM

The NWRO Budget is computed on the basis of surveys conducted by the Department of Labor's Bureau of Labor Statistics. These surveys, as reported in Labor Department Bulletin No. 1570-5 <u>Three Standards of Living for an Urban Family of Four Persons</u>, reflect the approximate amount of money that a family of four must spend for the "maintenance of health and social well-being, the nurture of children, and participation in community activities".

9

The report outlines three budgets at three different levels, lower, moderate and higher. NWRO's Adequate Income Budget is based primarily on the lower living standard budget which generally allows a family of four to have access to decent standards in housing, transportation, clothing and personal care.

However, we reject the lower living standard's food budget which is based on the U. S. Department of Agriculture's "low cost food plan". Government surveys show that 70% of the families with food budgets equivalent to the low-cost food plan have nutritionally inadequate diets. Therefore, the NWRO Budget uses the Agriculture Department's "moderate food plan" which would assure an adequate diet for every American. NWRO contends that providing an adequate income is the only way to combat hunger in America.

In calculating its budget NWRO specifically rejected the official Poverty Level as a measure of what a
family needs to live at a minimum adequate level.
The Poverty Level was devised by the Social Security Administration on the basis of the Agriculture Department's economy food plan. But the Agriculture Department has said that the economy
food plan "is not a reasonable measure of basic
money needs for a good diet.   The public assistance agency that recognizes the limitations of its
clientele and is interested in their nutritional well-
being, will recommend a money allowance for food
considerably higher than the cost level of the economy plan".

The Social Security Administration ignored the
USDA warning.   They took the cost level of the
economy plan and simply multiplied it by three to
determine the total "poverty level" budget for a
10 family of four. This procedure is made totally in-
appropriate because, in addition to the Agriculture
Department's own statement, the Bureau of Labor
Statistics has pointed out that a family of four has
a total budget closer to four or five times the cost
of it's food component.

The following table shows how the minimum adequate budget is broken down. The budget excludes
the basic cost of hospital and doctor's care, since
it is assumed that free medical care will be available through Medicaid, national health insurance
or some other program.

It should be carefully noted that this is a minimum
adequacy budget. It provides only a basic subsistence income.   There is no allowance for things
like life insurance, out-of-town travel, a car, ci-
garettes, long-distance phone calls, or use of a
laundromat.

CATEGORY	COST PER	YEAR	MONTH	WEEK
FOOD		$2630	$217	$50

This allowance is a total of the BLS Moderate Budget cost for food at home ($2351/yr., $195/mo., $48/wk.) and the BLS lower standard for food away from home ($279/yr., $23/mo., $6/wk.) The latter includes snacks, school lunches, etc.

| **HOUSING** | | 1648 | 137 | 32 |

These costs represent the BLS lower standard's costs, updated to spring 1969 levels. They are meant to cover all supplies and furnishings for the home and its operations including telephone and postage. Rental costs ($1303/yr.,$108/mo.) include all items like gas, elec., and water.

| **CLOTHING AND PERSONAL CARE** | | 922 | 76 | 18 |

The items in this budget, shampoo and yard goods as well as clothing and clothing care, are unchanged from the BLS lower standard. The cost has simply been updated to spring 1969 levels.

| **MEDICAL CARE** | | 367 | 30 | 7 |

Dental, eye care, and non-prescription drugs are included here. BLS consideration of doctor and hospital care has been omitted, as explained in the text. There is no provision for medical appliances and supplies.

| **TRANSPORTATION** | | 569 | 47 | 11 |

Includes school bus rides and all other use of public transportation by non-car owners.

| **OTHER** | | 379 | 32 | 7 |

Reading, recreation and education comprise about ½ of this category. There is no provision, according to the BLS study for life insurance, club membership dues, hobby expenses or the acquisition of musical instruments.

| **TOTAL** | | 6515 | 542 | 125 |

MINIMUM ADEQUATE BUDGET FOR A FAMILY OF FOUR

11

WHERE THE MONEY WOULD COME FROM

12

NWRO's Adequate Income Plan would provide benefits in the form of actual payments, work incentives or tax relief to a little over half the country's people. . . . 112 million, according to estimates made by the U.S. Department of Health, Education and Welfare. The Plan would cost about $60 billion more than we currently spend on welfare.

That sounds like a lot. It is a lot more than Congress is currently willing to spend on poor people. But it is not so much when you compare it to what Congress spends for war, spends for the rich and for the corporations.

There is a big welfare program now. . . welfare for defense contractors, welfare in the form of tax loopholes for the very rich and for the large companies, welfare for big farm corporations that do not plant crops. . . but there is very little welfare for the poor.

President Nixon is increasing welfare for the rich and cutting back welfare for the poor. He is underwriting big defense companies that can't make it on their own. He is increasing tax depletion allowances for corporations. His so-called welfare reform plan would actually reduce benefits for poor people on welfare. Ninety percent of the welfare families could receive lower benefits than they now receive. The few legal and Constitutional rights recipients now enjoy will be undermined and even mothers of small children will be forced to work away from home or be cut off assistance.

BUILDING THE FIGHT-BILL H.R. 7257

NWRO has begun the fight for adequate income. Other organizations have joined the struggle, including major religious, social welfare, and civic groups.

Twenty-one members of the House of Representatives, including the entire Black Congressional Caucus, have introduced H. R. 7257, a bill which would implement the NWRO $6500 Plan. Those Representatives include:

> Democrats: Charles B. Rangel, N.Y., Shirley Chisholm, N.Y., William L. Clay, Mo., George W. Collins, Ill., Ralph H. Metcalfe, Ill., Charles C. Diggs, Mich., Ronald V. Dellums, Calif., John Conyers, Jr., Mich., Augustus F. Hawkins, Calif., Louis Stokes, Ohio, Robert N.C. Nix, Penn., Bella Abzug, N.Y., Herman Badillo, N.Y., Benjamin S. Rosenthal, N.Y., William F. Ryan, N.Y., Ken Hechler, West Virginia, Abner J. Mikva, Ill., Melvin Price, Ill., Edward R. Roybal, Calif., Parren J. Mitchell, Md.
> Republican: Seymour Halpern, N.Y.

13

But H. R. 7257 is only a symbol of the work that lies ahead. The myths about welfare and welfare recipients must be destroyed and the priorities of our country must be reversed. If NWRO's Plan were enacted, the 20% of the people with the highest income would receive only 20% of the country's total income (instead of the 43% they get now). The bottom 20% would have about 15% instead of its present 6%. Poor people, middle-income people, all people who believe in dignity, justice, democracy and the right to an adequate income, must build the fight for $6500 NOW!

STEPS TOWARD TRUE WELFARE REFORM

1. ADEQUATE INCOME GOAL
Adequate income based on the NWRO $6500 standard should be made a national goal.

2. HIGHER FEDERAL FLOOR
The federal government should establish a floor on welfare benefits as close to $6500 as possible.

3. TIME TABLE
There should be a timetable for reaching adequate income at the earliest possible date.

4. EMERGENCY GRANTS
There should be emergency grants to bring people up to a decent standard when they go on the program and to take care of special or unusual circumstances.

5. COST-OF-LIVING INCREASES
There should be increases in the grant level to compensate for increases in the cost-of-living at least once a year.

6. INCLUDE ALL POOR PEOPLE
Coverage should be broadened to include all poor people, not just families with children.

14

7. SIMPLIFIED ADMINISTRATION
There should be one unified program operated by the federal government.

8. NO FORCED WORK
There should be no requirement making work or job training a requisite to receiving aid.

9. JOB STANDARDS
All jobs offered should be regulated by strict national standards including minimum wage and fair labor standards.

10. RECIPIENTS' RIGHTS
Recipients should receive a clear explanation of their rights and recipient organizations must be recognized as parties in legal action and be given copies of all regulations and procedures.

15

TO FIND OUT MORE ABOUT THE NWRO ADEQUATE INCOME PLAN CONTACT THE NATIONAL OFFICE, 1424–16th STREET, N.W., WASHINGTON, D.C. 20036. Telephone –(202) 483-1531.

☞ CHAPTER EIGHT
NOW:
WHAT CAN YOU DO TO CHANGE THE WELFARE SYSTEM?

Now that we know something about welfare—its structure, history, facts, myths, functions, welfare reform, alternatives—we should be ready to get our heads together. If you have read and reflected, if you have tried on and tried out the arguments and new-to-you ideas, if you have done some of the Do-its, then you have at least made a substantial start on developing an **analysis** of the welfare system. Chapter 7 should have already started you on the next important step—thinking about an **alternative** to the welfare system. What is left is figuring out a strategy of how to get from welfare-as-it-is to welfare-as-you-want-it-to-be.

Both to prepare to talk about that and by way of summing up and reviewing, let us look at some key issues.

I believe there are four central issues: money, work, the welfare contract, and welfare as an institution.

MONEY
Is there enough to go around? Should some people be rich and some hungry? Do we owe everyone/anyone a living? Can we afford adequate income for all? Should welfare **redistribute** income and wealth? Is anything else besides money needed to end poverty? If any **services** are needed/useful, what kinds? who should control them? should they be offered by both government and private agencies?

WORK
Is it still necessary? Is it an integral part of "the human condition"? What do most workers in our society **produce?** Should welfare be used to encourage/enforce work? If so, how? If not, how can welfare and work be creatively separated after their long "marriage"?

THE WELFARE CONTRACT
Gilbert Steiner puts the question succinctly: "The overriding policy conflict in public assistance is between those who would impose constraints on the behavior of relief recipients and those who focus on need as the sole issue." *

I have thought about this in two different ways:

1. No conditions: Birth is the only "requirement." The right to live is absolute.
2. My version of a "social contract": Each person receives an "adequate income" but in turn must contribute to society. (An earlier version is "from each according to his abilities to each according to his need.") Big problem: Who decides?

WELFARE AS AN INSTITUTION
Whether separated from work or not, whether some kind of "social" contract or simply a "right to live" the question still/ yet arises: what would the **function** of welfare in the society be? In addressing this I look at the earlier example (p. 121) where Winifred Bell's study found that AFDC "suitable home" policies had been used in the 1940s and '50s to keep black children off welfare. If by a **social institution** we mean simply a **pattern,** a way of doing things, then in this case the institution of welfare clearly helped support the institution we have come to identify as **racism.** This example leads me to three questions:

1. Do social institutions interrelate and support one another? If so, what about the relation between welfare and the family,

* Gilbert Y. Steiner, **Social Insecurity, The Politics of Welfare** (Chicago: Rand McNally & Co., 1966), p. 112. Used by permission.

sexism, and religion? How do these institutions interrelate?

2. If some institutions are used to **support** others, are some more important (in the sense of more basic) than others? Although welfare is the institution I am writing this book about (and thus is very important), aren't racism and war, for example, more basic and critical human behavior patterns?

3. To me the most serious question then becomes: if welfare is used to support racism what in turn is racism for? What is its **role,** its function? And if we answer this in general terms that racism is used to support "what is" (the status quo) then what kind of status quo is it? What kind of society are we that we **need** (or at least make use of) such institutions as welfare and racism and war?

Obviously each person must ask and answer these kinds of questions for himself/herself. For me, the answer to the last question is that something is radically (in the sense of at the **root**) wrong with such a society (ours). And so change is necessary.

Opal C. Jones, the director of the neighborhood center where I began my compensatory education when I left social work school, told me about a group she had worked with in Atlanta, Georgia. They called themselves T.I.C.—to improve conditions —and their motto was "something must be did." But what?

You may expect a lengthy, detailed prescription from me. After all, I have already made it clear that change is a passion of mine. I have been working at, studying, and thinking about change for almost ten years of my life. But after thinking for a while that I knew something about social change I have finally, in e.e. cummings' words, "trudged up to ignorance again!"

So, I can only offer a few guesses:

1. I think making change must involve shared effort. We need to aim at being "social changers" versus "change agents."
2. I think change must flow from shared ideas about **what is and what is needed.**
3. To make change you must begin.

In more concrete terms, I have only two complementary (free and fit together) suggestions:

First, support the National Welfare Rights Organization (NWRO).

As noted already, if there is anything **new** in the welfare situation, it is welfare recipients becoming organized, acting and speaking in their own behalf, defining their own interests.

Support means just that. They lead; we follow.

Ways to help include **money**, political support, public support, day-to-day volunteer work, babysitting, transportation, office work, etc.

One underrated form of support is simply to **recognize** that welfare recipients **have** an organization and to treat it with respect.

And support means of the organization **as it is** versus as we might like it to be. Some people don't like NWRO's **tactics**—others may question its ends. You can raise questions about NWRO but then decide whether or not you can support it and if the answer is yes—DO IT.

But support of the movement of poor people, third world people, oppressed people, as useful and necessary as it is—is not sufficient if in the movement phase we are to "free all political prisoners." Because **we**—middle Americans—are ourselves political prisoners. This is especially true regarding the welfare system. In William Ryan's terms again, we are involved with "reconciling our own self-interest with the promptings of humanitarian impulses." Who are we allowing to **define** our self-interest? the politicians? the media? the "corporate state machine" described by Charles Reich in **The Greening of America**? Let's get our consciousness together!

Recently a study reported that most Americans viewed **themselves** as getting ahead in terms of personal satisfaction with life and hope for the future. But they clearly feel the **nation** is in trouble. In fact, 47 percent believe unrest and ill-feeling is likely to lead to a real breakdown in this country! The country is likely to come apart but I'm o.k.! How can this be?

It can't be. Reality isn't simply personal; it is **social.** Things

SUPPORT YOUR LOCAL

WELFARE RIGHTS ORGANIZATION

FRIEND ∞ NWRO

NATIONAL
WELFARE RIGHTS ORGANIZATION
MEMBERSHIP RECORD

(Please Print)

Name_____

Mailing Address_____ Phone_____

City_____ State_____ Zip Code_____

Local Welfare Rights Group_____

Employed by_____ Title_____

Organization Affiliations_____

Date Joined_____Membership Paid $____ Pledge of $____per____

Received by_____

Special ways I think I can help NWRO:_____

_____

mail to: National Welfare Rights Organization
1424—16th Street, N.W.
Washington, D.C. 20036
Telephone—(202)483-1531

WHAT CAN YOU DO TO CHANGE THE WELFARE SYSTEM?

are not "fine" for you and me and bad for "them." At least not for me they aren't. I don't believe either that things in this country are basically o.k. but we just have a few minor problems, a little unfinished business (like poverty, racism, and war) to take care of.

I believe we middle Americans need to begin redefining our self-interest. I think we need to define it in **social** terms, in ecological terms, in humanistic terms.

Pogo once said "We have met the enemy and they are us." In the case of the welfare system, we middle Americans have probably been both enemy and victim. And if we remain silent or let George (whether Wiley, Wallace, or McGovern) do it, then we deserve it.

To paraphrase Rabbi Hillel:

If I am not for my own welfare, then who will be?

And if I am for my welfare alone, then what am I?

And if not now, when?

☛ DO-ITS

1. Argue about welfare with your beautician or barber, a cab driver, your parents, your neighbors.
2. DO IT.
3. See postscript.

POSTSCRIPT

Contrary to usual protocol, I wish to solicit feedback and response to this book. How else will I learn? Don't leave it to "the critics." Write and tell me if the book was in any way useful (or why not). What are you doing? What would you like to do?

with love

Tim Sampson
2237 Roosevelt, Apt. 2
Berkeley, California 94703